T26088

W9-CZO-188

PICKERING PUBLIC LIBRARY

3 3001 00066782 5

Kinsale Association
Library

c1

9
97

k3 c1

PICKERING PUBLIC LIBRARY
CENTRAL BRANCH

Library

THE MASSEYS/FOUNDING FAMILY

MOLLIE GILLEN

THE

MASSEYS

FOUNDING FAMILY

08850

THE RYERSON PRESS TORONTO

PICKERING PUBLIC LIBRARY
CENTRAL BRANCH

© THE RYERSON PRESS, 1965

PRINTED AND BOUND IN CANADA
BY THE RYERSON PRESS, TORONTO

ACKNOWLEDGMENTS

Writing this book has been a fascinating
experience, and its completion has meant, not
the end of the research but merely
abandonment of it, with the uncomfortable
feeling that so much more is still undiscovered.
I am grateful for permission to use the
material prepared for and published in
Chatelaine in June, July and August of 1964.
My thanks must also go to members of
the Massey family, who have been unfailingly
courteous and helpful, searching albums to
dig up the many wonderful photographs
from past and present; to Massey-Ferguson,
who allowed access to the company's
archives; to local residents in the Cobourg
area who received me kindly and directed me
to new sources of information; to friends
and acquaintances who gave me encouragement
and help; to my family, who put up with
neglected household chores; and to United
Church and Anglican Church archivists and
staff members of the Ontario Provincial
Archives and the Toronto Public Library,
particularly the gentlemen in the Toronto
Room, who uncomplainingly heaved around
for me dusty volumes of early Ontario
newspapers.
I hope all these people will feel that the final
result justifies their efforts.

M. G.

ILLUSTRATIONS

CONTENTS

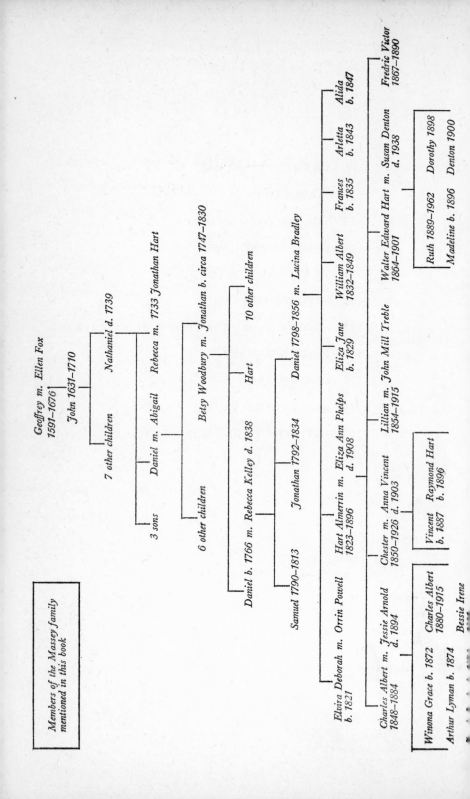

Members of the Massey family
mentioned in this book

Geoffrey m. Ellen Fox
1591–1676
John 1631–1710

7 other children   Nathaniel d. 1739

3 sons   Daniel m. Abigail   Rebecca m. 1733 Jonathan Hart

6 other children   Betsy Woodbury m. Jonathan b. circa 1747–1830

Daniel b. 1766 m. Rebecca Kelley d. 1838   Hart   10 other children

Samuel 1790–1813   Jonathan 1792–1834   Daniel 1798–1856 m. Lucina Bradley

Elvira Deborah m. Orrin Powell   Hart Almerrin m. Eliza Ann Phelps   Eliza Jane   William Albert   Frances   Arletta   Alida
b. 1821   1823–1896   d. 1908   b. 1829   1832–1849   b. 1835   b. 1843   b. 1847
                                                                                                         Fredric Victor
                                                                                                         1867–1890

Charles Albert m. Jessie Arnold   Chester m. Anna Vincent   Lillian m. John Mill Treble   Walter Edward Hart m. Susan Denton
1848–1884   d. 1894   1850–1926   d. 1903   1854–1915   1864–1901   d. 1938

Winona Grace b. 1872   Charles Albert   Vincent   Raymond Hart   Ruth 1889–1962   Dorothy 1898
Arthur Lyman b. 1874   1880–1915   b. 1887   b. 1896   Madeline b. 1896   Denton 1900
Bessie Irene

The Restless Years

~~Kinsale Association~~
Library

Long ago they were noblemen from France. One of them, Hamon de Macei, came over with William of Normandy to aid in the conquest of England. Then they were younger sons without estates drifting into humbler occupations. Later they were farmers and pioneers, respected citizens in new communities, building their lives in another land across a wider ocean. One of them set himself up as a founder, in a small village workshop that grew into an industrial giant. Today they are prominent in other worlds than those of war and commerce: the worlds of diplomacy, letters, architecture, theatre. The Massey energy and Massey initiative drive them yet.

There would have been one precise moment, an exact and definite point of time when the decision was taken by a Massey to leave England for a new land where a man could follow the dictates of his own conscience, but the idea had been growing for years.

Twice in 1625 Geoffrey Massy, of Knutsford in Cheshire, had been required to appear before the courts of the church, once with his wife Ellen Fox (of Hunsterson in the parish of Wybunbury) and once alone, and confess to unacceptable behaviour. In an age of religious restlessness, when the devout who chafed under the established discipline of the church were often coerced and persecuted by the devout who were fighting to retain it, an escape route was open. Only five years earlier, in 1620, the Pilgrim Fathers had sailed for the new colony of Massachusetts across the Atlantic. To Geoffrey and his wife Ellen the enormous

1

undertaking of a transatlantic journey began to loom as a growing possibility.

Letters of dispensation for the marriage of the young couple had been issued on May twenty-fifth, 1625, to either the vicar or curate of Wybunbury or the curate of Nantwich, with one William Preston standing surety. The date of the subsequent marriage has been lost but there is evidence, since they were required to appear before the ecclesiastical judge on November fourth, that the church considered them to be living in sin. They were, however, the only couple in the five covered by the general indictment (uncompromisingly headed "Fornicators") who were referred to as man and wife, and it is possible that they were married by a dissenting minister not recognized by the church.

This would be offence enough. The church had been deeply disturbed for some time by what it considered the rapid deterioration in the moral climate of England (a concern not unfamiliar today, nor indeed in any period of the world's history). Already in the year 1590 a group of "Preachers in the Cowntie of Lancaster" were shaking their heads sadly over the "manifolde Enormities of the Ecclesiasticall state":

Divers maried in privat houses withoute any Bandes asked . . . or any Intelligence thereof geven to the Minister of the Churche. . . . The youthe will not by any means be brought to attende the Exercise of Catechizinge in the Afternoone: neither the people to be presentt at the Eveninge Service . . . Many Commers to the Churche, refuse to Communicat . . . Trienniall visitations . . . voide of all validitie and good effecte. What may be done for the reformation of these manifold Enormities, knowe we not.

It is no wonder that the church had begun to tighten its grip by calling to account recalcitrant parishioners like Geoffrey and Ellen Massy.

When he was called to appear Geoffrey pleaded illness and sent a friend to speak for him. In a strange mixture of debased

Latin and the English of the day, the ancient records of the church have preserved the story:

George Hurst appeared before the venerable . . . judge . . . and alleged that Geoffrey Massy was so affected by strange airs that he could not conveniently appear, wherefore he sought an order to be decreed as to the said Massy and Ellen Massy his wife. The judge enjoined "that they shold Confesse their falts in their Customed apparrell at divine service tyme some soundaie or hollie daie in Wibunbury or Knuttesford where the said Massy now dwelleth and so Certifie" before the next feast of Purification.

A marginal note adds in Latin: "Geoffrey Massy and his wife were dismissed because they confessed the charge according to the order decreed and the order remains with the certificate on the file." Perhaps confessing seemed the easy way out.

The second recorded occasion on which Geoffrey was in trouble with the church occurred at the end of the same month. In November he was one of twenty parishioners brought to answer to a charge of "receiving the Communion sitting," when the judge enjoined them "to receyve the holie and blessed Communion reverentlie knelinge att there owne churche and to certefye within two monthes next."

Geoffrey Massy (the name is variously spelled Geffraye, Jeffery, Goffray, and Massey appears as Massy, Massie, even Massyr) was an Elizabethan. He grew up in the age of Shakespeare and Laud when the creative genius of the civilized world that had burst from the dark loam of the Middle Ages was proving too hardy a growth to succumb to the futile cruelty of religious reactionaries. His baptism in December, 1591, is recorded in the parish register of Saint John the Baptist's Church in Knutsford in the Diocese of Chester in the County of Cheshire, only three years after the bonfires had flamed from hilltop to hilltop up the length of England with the news of the Armada's rout. In 1603 a new monarch became king of England, and a distinguished French explorer named Samuel de Champlain made his first voyage to that part of the North American continent called Canada, or "village," by an obscure tribe of

Indians. Young Geoffrey was almost twelve when his father, another Geoffrey, died in August of that year, leaving a will listing him as "householder" and bequeathing the bulk of his estate to his wife and children.

Geoffrey Massy could trace his pedigree to Hamon Macei (or Mascye), vassal of Hugh Lupus, a Norman noble who granted Hamon various lands on his vast Cheshire estates, and it has been deduced that he was probably a member of the family of Massey of Sale. His father, the elder Geoffrey, is thought to have been a shoemaker: economic pressures often forced the descendants of the younger sons of small squires into occupations and ways of life foreign to their original class. The younger Geoffrey was to carry an old name across a perilous ocean and give it a New World significance that would astonish him today.

The year 1625 had seen the death of a monarch who gave the world the King James Bible, but whose overtures to the Catholics had disturbed many of his sturdy subjects. The immediate and protracted quarrels with parliament about money and religion of his son Charles I gave little reason for optimism to those who hoped for religious freedom in England. Memories of the St. Bartholomew's Day massacre of the Huguenots in 1572 had not yet faded. The armies of the Thirty Years' War, begun in 1618, were marching and counter-marching across the map of Europe. The prolonged threat of a Catholic victory poised an uneasy sword above the heads of Protestants, and especially Puritans. A country gentleman named Oliver Cromwell, like Geoffrey Massy with unhappy memories of church discipline in 1621 and 1628, sold his property in Huntingdon in 1631 and rented instead: perhaps he, too, was thinking seriously of emigration.

Exactly when the young Massys made their momentous journey is not recorded. Many years later, the seventy-three-year-old Geoffrey would state in a deposition (on November thirtieth,

1664) that he had lived in Salem, Massachusetts, for about thirty-four years. It had been thirty-four years earlier, in June, 1630, that Governor John Winthrop had headed a group of almost a thousand emigrants who sailed for North America under a charter as "The Governor and Company of the Massachusetts Bay in New England." It seems likely that the decision of Geoffrey and Ellen, doubtless discussed for many a long night as candlelight and firelight flickered over earnest faces in a small English cottage, was implemented at that time. The town of Salem was only four years old in 1630; and new-settler Geoffrey, one of the first "layers-out of land for the towne" and proud father of a first son, John, born in Salem in 1631, had been admitted a freeman by 1634.

Geoffrey was a pillar of the community in the New World as perhaps he could never have been in the Old. In 1638 and 1639 he was one of the early deputies to the General Court of the Colonies. In 1640 he was appointed "to be an auditor and survey the books of the towne." He was eighty-five when he died, a respected citizen, in 1676.

A legend has arisen, in some places stated flatly as a fact, that what became the State of Massachusetts (actually named for the Massachusetts Indians) got its name from the prolific Masseys. The family did indeed proliferate and moved with the expanding frontiers of America, leaving sons and daughters to raise families of their own in the settlements of Massachusetts, New Hampshire, Vermont and New York. The genealogy of the North American Masseys, in fact, reads rather like a chapter of biblical "begats."

Geoffrey's son John, "one of ye first persons that was borne in this Towne of Salem of ye English nation," became an innholder, erecting on a lot of five acres the building known for a hundred years as the Ferry Tavern, and becoming ferry-master in 1686 at a new location. He died in 1710, "an upright man" aged seventy-nine. His eighth and youngest child Nathaniel, a cooper, bought out the rights of two sisters and a brother in their father's estate.

Nathaniel's will mentions four sons, to all of whom he left sections of his property on his death in 1739 (a daughter, Rebecca, who married one Jonathan Hart in 1733, predeceased her father). The two younger boys, Daniel and Samuel, got an odd deal: they were bequeathed half each of their father's "now dwelling house to the middle of the stack of chimney, leaving the entryway and stair in common," and half the orchard each on his own side of the house. They were also given a responsibility: to look after their uncle John "handsomely and well during his natural life and bury him decently."

The division of ownership, naturally enough, did not work well. Daniel, a ferryman, soon sold his share of the property, packed up as his great-grandfather Geoffrey had done, and set off around 1747 with his wife Abigail and young family to become one of the founders of New Salem in New Hampshire, where he built a house "on the north side of the road near Wilson's Corner towards the Causeway." The Massey gift for leadership made him a natural choice for selectman in 1759 and 1760. His seventh and youngest child Jonathan had a family of twelve: it was the eldest of the twelve, another Daniel, grandson of ferryman Daniel and sixth-generation descendant of immigrant Geoffrey, who left his home in Vermont to move across the border to Canada somewhere around the year 1802.

Daniel Massey's father Jonathan had been born just before his parents moved from Salem, Massachusetts, to Salem, New Hampshire. Here Jonathan married Betsey Woodbury, fathered his twelve children, and remained until 1792. He was sufficiently a son of his native land to take up arms in her defence against the British, serving first with the New Hampshire militia and in 1776 as a lieutenant with the Continental Army in the American Revolutionary War. His eldest son Daniel, who married Rebecca Kelley in 1787, was twenty-six and father of a two-year-old son when his forty-five-year-old father and forty-four-year-old mother

6

gathered up their brood in 1792 and departed on yet another westward journey, this time to Windsor, Vermont.

Jonathan's sons were as restless—or as adventurous—as their father. When a sturdy contemporary tourist named Jonathan Baker went on a walking tour in 1800, he found two cabins in the wilderness of upstate New York. One belonged to Zachariah Butterfield, the other to Daniel Massey. In March of the same year Daniel was joined by his younger brother Hart (was he named for his great-uncle by marriage, Jonathan Hart?) who stayed to become, with Butterfield and Henry Coffeen, a co-founder of the city of Watertown. In 1802 (after brief sojourns in other Vermont towns), father Jonathan followed his sons to live there until his death in 1830 at the age of eighty-three. But Daniel was not yet ready to put down roots. The same year found him on the move once more, this time to bring a branch of the North American Masseys under the British crown again.

With his wife Rebecca and three young sons—twelve-year-old Samuel, ten-year-old Jonathan and Daniel, four—Daniel Massey loaded his family goods on board a schooner and set out from Sackett's Harbour, New York, across Lake Ontario to the vicinity of Cobourg in Upper Canada (now Ontario). At that time there were more settlers in neighbouring Haldimand Township than in Cobourg itself (then known as Hamilton and renamed to mark the marriage in 1816 of Princess Charlotte, only child of the Prince Regent, to Prince Leopold of Saxe-Coburg). The Masseys may have landed at Carrying Place, Bay of Quinte, and travelled by wagon the forty-odd miles to their future homestead. If they landed at Cobourg, they came ashore in small boats and found themselves in a flat low area of cedar swamp from which they had to transport their household effects and farm implements some seven miles to the gentle hills of Haldimand Township. Here, just above the settlement first known as Grover's Tavern and named the village of Grafton in 1832, Daniel's first homestead was established.

Many years later, in 1857, the *Cobourg Star* would recall the scene at Cobourg as it had been when Zaccheus Burnham, a famous son of the town, first saw it in 1799:

... then covered with dense forest, not a single log cabin raised as a landmark in this dreary wilderness. The only "clearance" was a beaver meadow on the skirts of the little creek in the heart of the town. . . . Here Mr. Burnham cut his first hay, before grass had time to grow on the blackened fallow which the axe, the fire, and his own sturdy hands had cleared.

Sawmills and grist-mills had been built in 1798 where Port Hope now stands: around 1801 a grist-mill was established at Amherst, the earliest of the names by which Cobourg was known. One Eliud Nickerson was the first settler in the district, living in a "crude wood hut" on a lot for which he got his deed in 1802.

Daniel's name is not recorded as a purchaser of land until 1812, when he bought one hundred and ten acres in the third concession back from the lake front, but the census rolls for 1808 show a clear picture of the little family. Probably renting part of the land he later bought, Daniel Massey at the age of forty-two held thirty acres of land under cultivation, with seventy acres as yet unworked, his property valued at £82. Here, in a house of round logs, Daniel lived the hard life of a frontier farmer with his wife and family, now including three small daughters. He owned three horses, four oxen and two milch cows. Young Daniel, now ten, was almost as useful around the farm as his older brothers, Samuel, a sturdy eighteen, and Jonathan, sixteen in July, 1808. In fact, when the War of 1812 began, calling father Daniel and probably the two older boys into its service, young Daniel at fourteen was left to manage the farm alone.

In those days a boy was expected very early to carry a man's responsibilities. At the age of six, long before he was ready to be dispatched to the Watertown, New York, home of his grandfather Jonathan for three years of schooling, Daniel already had his own small duties. A boy only four or five years old could bring in water, carry firewood, drive the cattle to pasture. Above all, he could discover self-reliance and the importance of justice and duty. By the time father Daniel went off to drive a team for the Canadian militia, young Daniel was already an experienced manager. At harvest time he employed the necessary farmhands, settled the accounts, took the grain to market. Handicapped by the loss of the young farm horses to the army, he broke in two young steers to take their place. Once, when offered by a speculator what he considered too low a price for a load of poultry, he harnessed up the one elderly remaining horse and carted the whole lot seventy miles to Kingston, a journey certainly difficult and possibly dangerous. The Danforth Road, built by American contractor Asa Danforth between the years 1798 and 1800 at a price of $90 a mile, had been opened from Kingston as far west as Ancaster, near Hamilton, but between settlements it soon tended to go back to little more than a blazed path through the woods.

Young Daniel had undertaken a big responsibility for a fourteen-year-old. The air was alive with menacing stories of American invasion. Did they hear, in the backwoods of Haldimand Township, of the feverish activity in Sackett's Harbour across the lake where the Americans were gathering ships and men for the invasion of York at the end of April, 1813? Certainly they saw the retreating British soldiers who straggled up the road to Kingston, "leaving wounded in every farmhouse." The weather was dreadful. A continuous downpour turned the barely thawed ground into a quagmire, making bad roads almost impassable. By April thirtieth Major-General Sheaffe and the British had reached Haldimand, where he stopped over. Foot soldiers, who endured the cold and the rain without shelter or food or conveyance, would not easily forget the nightmare journey. It was on May third, just after the invasion, that Daniel's older brother Samuel died at the age of twenty-three. He was buried in the small cemetery on Academy Hill a mile or so from the homestead, and here his tombstone still stands. Was he, too, a victim of the War of 1812?

9

The year's planting and harvest were both completed when Daniel senior returned to take charge once more. In 1814 his second son Jonathan went off to a farm of his own nearby, with a young bride, Rachel Merrill (a great-grandson, Grant Massey, still farms the same lot with his son Carman). Daniel, according to the traditions of the day, owed his services to his father until he was twenty-one. In 1817, when only nineteen, Daniel asked his father to release him, forfeiting all claims to his share of the estate in return, and moved to rented land in the neighbourhood to start out on his own. But for the next two years Daniel did little farming. He had developed an interest in clearing wild lands. Since help was easy to find among the immigrants flocking to Upper Canada from Britain, this proved to be a profitable project.

The problem at that time was not conservation but how quickly the land could be cleared. Daniel's work would raise the value of the land for its owners, and the lumber would bring a good price in an area that needed wood for its barns, its houses and its furniture, its fence posts and farm implements, its corduroy roads, culverts, bridges and its winter fuel.

Roads throughout the area were little more than tracks among the trees, with logs laid crosswise over the swampy parts. The Kingston Road, completed by 1817, was the first really usable road, and a weekly stage service was begun in January of that year between Kingston and York (now Toronto), with a fare of eighteen dollars for the three-day trip. The half-way point was Spalding's Inn at Grafton, the nearest settlement to Daniel's modest property. The Haldimand district had more than six thousand acres under cultivation (valued at from ten to fifteen shillings an acre), and there were three grist mills and four sawmills.

By 1820, twenty-two-year-old Daniel, a determined young man with a jutting jaw and piercing eyes, owned several parcels of land in the rolling countryside above Cobourg. Registers of deeds contain the complicated story of his sales and purchases almost

10

impossible to follow, as lots were broken into smaller parcels and joined to other lots. He had married, in January, 1820, a childhood sweetheart, Lucina Bradley, whose grandfather Nathan had left Illinois in 1777 with his wife Elizabeth and infant son William and eventually settled in Haldimand Township. They had fled from their home when they saw Indians approaching, Nathan carrying the baby and supporting his wife with his arm as they forded a river. On a hilltop they looked back to see their house in flames.

Daniel and Lucina set up housekeeping in "a house of squared or hewed timber," equipped with home-made furniture and "two additional fireplaces." In 1821 they had their first child, a girl they named Elvira Deborah. On April twenty-ninth, 1823, a son was born and named Hart Almerrin—the Hart for Daniel's uncle, co-founder and now respected citizen of Watertown, New York.

For the next ten years lumbering and land-clearing kept Daniel busy, and he attacked the various problems with the vigour and initiative he had shown as a boy. When everyone else was getting rid of useless timber by laboriously rolling the logs with handspikes into piles for burning, Daniel hastened the process by using teams of oxen. He became so expert in land-clearing, indeed, that he was asked to prepare a paper on the subject (later published).

Over the years to 1830, Daniel cleared twelve hundred acres of timberland, employing as many as a hundred men at a time. These he would find by riding—or quite often, walking—to the nearest lake ports and selecting the best available men as they landed. With no real harbour facilities in Cobourg until 1830, immigrants came ashore in small boats to the landing wharf. Often as many as two thousand people came in at one time, and the beach would be covered with small white tents. An observer of the day thought they made a very pretty sight dotted along the shore.

Daniel's son followed the pattern of his father's own childhood, making himself useful almost from the time he could walk. As a barefoot youngster of seven, it was young Hart's duty to go on horseback once a week to the grist-mill four miles away and bring back the ground grain. He was too small to handle the logs used for fuel in the house, but with someone in the woods to load and someone at home to unload, Hart would drive the team and drag the logs from the woods to the sawmill on his father's property. A year later he was going to the local distillery for the weekly supply of five gallons of whisky for the hired hands, the keg slung over his horse and balanced by a stone on the other side. Daniel took the boy along with him on his business trips, buying and selling cattle and marketing grain. By the time Hart was ten, he could handle this responsibility almost alone. With one of the men along to move the heavy bags, Hart took charge of the oxen, sold the produce, and cashed his father's cheques at the Bank of Montreal in Cobourg.

In 1824 the first clergyman of the Methodist congregation in Cobourg, the Reverend Anson Green, reported that the town had "a hundred inhabitants with two small stores, several mechanics and plenty of taverns." By 1832 the population had risen to a thousand, and there were a hundred and fifty houses, twenty stores, three taverns, two schools, three surgeons, an apothecary. A solid courthouse and an impressive Anglican church with a belfry gave dignity to the town. Young Hart, arriving there early in the day, would find the stir and bustle of business already in full swing. People went to work at sunrise (in summer as early as 4:30 A.M.), and breakfast in the taverns was served at six o'clock, a hearty meal for the work of the day ahead, with tea, coffee and toast, the "never-failing buckwheat cakes," various sweetmeats and a dish of beefsteak and onions. Cobourg had its first fire-engine in 1832, and the *Cobourg Star* had published its first issue on January eleventh, 1831. Among its other news items was a report of the County of Northumberland Agricultural Society, noting that Hart's uncle Jonathan had produced the

12

second-best acre of potatoes with four hundred and thirty bushels, and the information that a letter awaited his father Daniel at the post office.

Up to now Daniel had followed the local custom of supplying whisky to the farm workers, though his Methodist principles had always been affronted by the practice. Now he took the risk of a firmer stand. When the growing temperance movement in the United States came to his notice, he made up his mind. "From now on," he declared, "no more liquor on my premises."

In a day when life was rough and hard, cheap beer and whisky offered a form of escape and excitement. Daniel had made an unpopular decision. His first difficulty occurred at a barn raising: the men refused to work without liquor. Daniel hired some sailors with block and tackle and got the work done in less time with fewer hands. But a more serious crisis came at harvest time. The muttering among the men turned to open revolt. When Daniel faced them in the fields, they looked across the acres of grain swaying gold in the sunlight, and threatened blackmail. "Your grain will rot," they told him, "unless we get our whisky."

"If it takes whisky to save it," Daniel said defiantly, "the grain may go back to the ground before I will furnish the stuff."

To small Hart, holding his breath as he listened, his eyes going from the men's flushed faces to Daniel's set lips, his father seemed a hero of biblical proportions. He was well aware how much of their livelihood hung on the results of the harvest. "Saddle the horses," Daniel said. "We'll get other men to do the job." Father and son rode to Cobourg, where a shipload of immigrants had just arrived. Young Hart must have thought it the proper reward of virtue when from among the newcomers a crew was found who knew the use of scythe and sickle. The harvest was garnered, and without whisky.

On a hot bright August day in 1834, Daniel's brother Jonathan was killed at the age of forty-two by an accident at a Saturday barn raising. It had been a day of excitement and chatter, the women of the district arriving with the young children to prepare food and exchange gossip, the men and older boys working on the building, sometimes dividing into teams that would challenge each other in a race to get one end up before the other. Daniel and Lucina loaded their farm cart with children and supplies and drove over to Jonathan's farm early in the morning. Hart joined his father and uncle and five male cousins outdoors. Lucina and her daughters Elvira, Elizabeth and Eliza Jane joined Rachel and her three girls in the kitchen. Work proceeded happily and noisily until tragedy struck. One of the workers, who had taken too much of the free liquor, dropped a handspike that felled Jonathan instantly. As the sobered crowd gathered round, the critically injured man was carried to the house. Though he managed to dictate a most competent will that left his widow and his eight surviving children properly cared for, he was unable to sign it with more than a mark. He died next day. Eleven-year-old Hart, wide-eyed and appalled, needed no further example to make him a lifelong and active campaigner for temperance.

At six, Hart had gone off with his older sister Elvira to the small schoolhouse three miles away on Academy Hill. The two children would drive the cattle to pasture in the morning and drive them back again in the afternoon as they returned from school. The teacher had few qualifications, and the children received only sketchy instruction. In the winter of 1834 Hart was sent to stay with one of his father's uncles in Watertown, New York. There he had his first unbroken year of school.

The Canadian Masseys had always kept in close touch with the Watertown Masseys. In winter months, when he could be spared from the farm, Daniel would pack Lucina and the children into the sleigh and cross the St. Lawrence on the ice for family visits and business deals. Always intrigued by innovations, his eye was caught on one of these visits in 1830 (the year his grandfather Jonathan died in Watertown) by a machine he had never seen

14

before, a mechanical thresher. With a growing family (Elizabeth had been born in 1827 and Eliza Jane in 1829) and most of the land in the area now cleared, Daniel was ready to settle down to full-time farming. His shrewd eyes at once saw the advantages of such a machine over the laborious manpower methods unchanged through recorded history. At considerable trouble and expense he had one transported across Lake Ontario and set up in his barn.

Before the introduction of farm machinery the grain, gathered with sickle and cradle, had been threshed in the barn by flail or by driving cattle over it. The new machine, clumsy, stationary, and requiring the labour of a dozen men, still managed to pay for itself by threshing grain for neighbouring farmers. Daniel prowled round his captive monster, watching the grain fall away from the stalks in a steady stream, his quick mind suddenly aware of limitless possibilities. He examined every detail of the implement, crawling and poking to find out why this cog was needed here, what purpose this lever served, what made that wheel rotate, marvelling that no one had come up with such an idea before. If threshing could be done mechanically, why not reaping? Why not binding? And why import these machines? Could they not be made here, in Upper Canada? What leaping visions did practical Daniel have to hold in check behind that dour no-nonsense face, what flashing excitement sparked in his blood while he went about his chores? Patient Lucina must have listened a hundred times to Daniel's impossible dreaming as she did her household tasks in the same old way, nursing her babies, putting up fruit and vegetables, washing and baking and spinning.

By 1834 Daniel had added several hundreds of acres to his property in the second concession above Cobourg (later known as the Gully district), and his farm was one of the largest and best cultivated in the area. The homestead stood high above the surrounding land, a spacious frame building two storeys high in the centre, with a one-storey wing on either side. On every visit to Watertown Daniel's sharp eyes discovered new devices,

15

which eventually made their appearance on the Haldimand farm. The "bull thresher" was replaced by a lighter portable model. Improved harrows, new-fangled ploughs, a fanning mill were brought in—not without some local opposition. As in every age, men feared the machine that could replace them. One of the early reapers imported by a progressive neighbour was set on fire and burned in the fields by the farmhands.

Though the settlers in the backwoods and the residents of the fast-growing country towns had their own spirited social life, growing out of the necessity for neighbourly co-operation and built on a human interest in the doings of their immediate fellows, they were intensely eager for news of the world they had left. The *Cobourg Star* catered to both needs. In 1831 it was requested to announce "that the large *dog* belonging to Mr. Truman Hinman, of Haldimand, that has so long been an annoyance to the public, has been destroyed by that gentle-man." It recorded the marriage at Queenston, in November, 1833, of Miss Laura, daughter of James Secord, Esquire, to Mr. John Poore, first cousin of the late Sir Isaac Brock and, in the following week, of the Reverend Egerton Ryerson to Miss Mary Armstrong. It was also to note, on July twenty-eighth, six years later, the death of the youngest son of Captain John Poore. These were days when infant mortality was heartbreakingly high and often the death notices had to record the loss of three children in a family within one week.

On July second, 1834, the *Star* announced breathlessly: "Lafayette is dead!" In 1836 it noted the death of Lieutenant-Colonel John By at his residence in England, and of Marie Laetitia Bonaparte, mother of Napoleon, in Rome. It gravely drew to its readers' attention a marriage in New Orleans of one Alexander Philip Socrates Amelius Caesar Hanibal Marcellus George Washington Treadwell and Miss Caroline Sophia Maria Wortley Montague Joan of Arc Williams, "all of that city." It carried "announcements" of wide interest: "A beautiful mare, rising five years old, warranted to run in double or single harness and to plough kindly . . ."; the opening of the Cobourg Circulating Library, "7/6 for 3 months, 13/6 for 6 months, £1/5/- for one year, produce taken in payment." (Ten years later another circulating library was established by one Charles Boyer.) It applauded the appearance of Chang-Eng, the Siamese twins, of whom a likeness could be bought for 12½¢, or at 25¢ a lithograph for framing; and a one-day visit of the Zoological Institute of New York, with "elephant, gnu, condor, white pelicans, black-maned Cape lion, zebra, leopards, hyena, camels, crested porcupine, zebu, peruvian foxes, man-monkey, talking parrots, etc. . . . also collection of Paintings, also Boa Constrictor and Anaconda, 7½d. per person, children under ten half-price."

And beneath the surface of recorded events Daniel Massey pursued his busy round of activities, his name emerging out of anonymity into the columns of the *Cobourg Star* just often enough over the years to allow a tantalizing glimpse of a man well integrated into the society of his time and place:

A letter is being held at the post office for Daniel Massey. . . . The prayer of Daniel Massey and others to the Newcastle District Council was not complied with. . . . The Newcastle Hounds will meet . . . Tuesday next at Mr. Daniel Massey's, Haldimand . . . at 8 o'clock a.m. A letter . . . for Daniel Massey . . .

The postal services of the day were not satisfactory to everyone. "I live in a retired part of the Country," wrote a gentleman named Dick, to the *Star* of February tenth, 1836, "and therefore do not hear much of what passes in Town. I have understood, however, that you have such a thing as a Post Office in Cobourg. And, under the impression that such was the case, I have been in the habit, whenever I came to Town, of going to the house pointed out to me as the said office; but have never yet found it open, or a soul inside. Perhaps the worthy Post Master is in the habit of going hunting or driving during

17

the day, and has a fashion of dealing out the letters during the night. Would you be good enough to let me know whether this is the case or not; as I should not mind paying for a night's lodging, or appointing an agent to wait upon his 'mightiness', for the sake of getting my letters, which I am sure must have been some time in the office."

Eighty-three of his fellow-townsmen had more faith in their postmaster than Dick did. He was triumphantly vindicated a month later by a letter over the signature of all of them.

Farm and Family

The years between 1830 when he imported his first mechanical implement and 1844, when he gave over the management of the farm to Hart and built himself a workshop where he could putter with machines to his heart's content, were prosperous years, though uneventful, for Daniel Massey—uneventful except for the joys and sorrows of his personal life. Two more sons were born, William Albert in 1832 and Jonathan in 1836, and two daughters, Frances (1835) and Lucina (1839). In 1837 little Elizabeth died, not quite ten, and Jonathan lived only for nine months. Baby Lucina disappeared quietly without record, mourned only by her family. Grandfather Daniel, the immigrant, died in 1832. His widow, Rebecca, lived to be seventy-three and was buried in January, 1838, in the cemetery across from the Academy Hill schoolhouse.

Young Hart was growing into a tall lean boy with prominent cheekbones, alternating his schooling between Watertown and Haldimand Township, meeting expenses by working on a relative's farm for fifty cents a day and risking the hazards that lay in wait for the people of the backwoods. Bears were numerous; ten or twelve were shot near Rice Lake, to the north, in 1836, "one she-bear swimming across the lake with two cubs on her back." The *Star* continually reported "horrid accidents," persons lost, drowned, found frozen.

During Hart's fifteenth year, when he was at Upper Canada Academy in Cobourg—later Victoria College—he cut wood and acted as fireman in the local tannery. In the summer months he worked on the farm, helping his father with the repair of the machines, at which he showed an uncanny ability.

19

When he was sixteen he borrowed two teams of oxen from his father, and at a logging camp in the woods began to acquire that skill in the management of men that would be one of the factors in his later success.

Daniel's heart must have been full when he looked at his eldest son. Hart was another Daniel: energetic, enterprising, decisive, he had early shown his father's conviction and interest in religion. The Masseys in the New World had all maintained their strong puritan principles as members of the nonconformist Baptist and Methodist churches (Jonathan in Salem, New Hampshire, was known as "Deacon": Watertown's Hart helped erect the First Presbyterian Church there in 1821). At fifteen, Hart decided to arrange services in his father's home, since distance, rough roads and lack of transport were keeping attendance poor at the bi-monthly Methodist service held in the log schoolhouse. Preachers spoke wherever a place could be found, in barns, sawmills, tanneries, private homes. Hart led the class, rounding up members and visiting absentees. It was no wonder that despite his youth he was elected steward and member of the quarterly board, beginning an active association with the church that would last for fifty-eight years.

With such rigid concepts of moral duty Hart Massey grew to manhood, motivated by his own acceptance of them, seldom coerced by stronger minds. Only once, ill and homesick in Watertown when he was sixteen, Hart's inflexible sense of duty wavered, bending to the sympathetic suggestion of a teacher that he take a trip home. After a stage journey of a hundred and fifty miles, he collapsed into the welcoming arms of his mother. Daniel was less than pleased: such self-indulgence was not in his code. The boy went back to Watertown by return stage.

The year 1844 was an important one for Hart. He turned twenty-one on April twenty-ninth, took over the farm management from his father and graduated from Victoria College under

20

President Egerton Ryerson. "On Thursday," said the *Cobourg Star* of May fifteenth, "the public reading of Essays, by young men of the Victoria College took place in the Methodist Chapel . . . on the whole very creditable . . . We observed several whose youth gives promise of a glorious manhood of intellect . . . and are likely to go forth . . . adding names which will shine in the list of Canada's rising talent."

On his twenty-first birthday, Daniel had taken his son aside to discuss the future.

"Now you're a man, Hart. What are your plans?"

"They are not clearly defined," Hart replied, "and I'd like your advice."

"Well," said Daniel, "you've shown great mechanical skill and you know how to manage men. There'll be increasing opportunities for making and selling farming tools in the city of Chicago. If you'd like to move there, I'll give you one thousand dollars. If you'd rather stay here, I'll give you a hundred and fifty acres of land. But if I were you, I'd go."

Hart may have considered the attractions of Chicago, but Lucina's was the deciding voice. "Please stay, Hart," his mother begged. "I can't bear to have you leave me." Hart's granite exterior was veined with tenderness: he stayed, and gave his usual wholehearted attention to the business of being a farmer. His father, freed from this responsibility, was now able to give all his time and attention to his workbench and forge.

The farm he handed over to his son's management was assessed in 1845 at a value of £806, with a one-storey building of hewn logs (Daniel's workshop), a two-storey frame house "with three additional fireplaces," eleven horses, twelve oxen, twelve cows, twenty-two calves and "one pleasure waggon."

By now Cobourg was a thriving and attractive place, busy with commerce, proud of its harbour facilities, its many fine public buildings and churches, good hotels and the active cultured life centred around Victoria College. Here the lively young Masseys became involved in community affairs and made

21

PICKERING TOWNSHIP PUBLIC LIBRARY
ROUGE HILL

their friendships. No doubt they took part in the 1840 celebrations for the marriage of the young Queen and her German prince, when triumphal arches were erected, flags flown on all houses, and military parades and firework displays organized all over the country. In Port Hope, pieces of an enormous bride-cake were distributed among the crowd. In 1840, too, the Grand Menagerie was back, announcing that the Giraffe, or Camel-Leopard, bought at a cost of £20,000, had died after shipping but was well-preserved, and that "the keeper will enter the den of lions, tigers, etc., and fondle them." The show was advertised as "suitable for the most refined and religious communities, and would instruct rather than traduce the nobler qualities of the mind."

On March tenth, 1842, Hart's sister Elvira had been married to Orrin Wentworth Powell of Cobourg, by a brother of Egerton Ryerson. Elvira had met her future husband when, bridesmaid at a local wedding, she found herself stranded, after Hart and the young brother of the best man ran off with the Massey buggy (perhaps this was the "pleasure waggon" listed as one of Daniel's assets). To his intense disgust, the best man had to drive Miss Massey home. Over the seven miles of country road, however, his reluctance quickly vanished. It was not long before Elvira was asking her father if young Mr. Orrin Powell of Cobourg might come courting.

"Not if he's like his old dad," Daniel snapped, rubbing his ear as he recalled the senior Powell's endless political harangues whenever they met. But gentle Orrin was not like his old dad, and he won his bride. Orrin and Elvira, whose wedding was held at the big frame house on the hill, were to celebrate a golden and a diamond anniversary and give two notable grandsons to Canada: Sir Edward Beatty, president of the Canadian Pacific Railway from 1918 to 1943, and Major-General Victor Odlum who, among other services to his country, officially represented Canada in Australia, China and Turkey.

Like the Masseys, the Powells had American cousins, the Phelps. When a Phelps cousin's early-winter wedding drew Orrin and Elvira to Gloversville, New York, in 1846, Hart decided to take the trip with them in the cutter. But at this wedding there were no tricks with buggies for Hart. He was far too busy trying to catch the attention of one of the guests, the prettiest girl he had ever seen.

Up to the day she died (at eighty-five in 1908), Eliza Ann Phelps kept her gentle beauty. She was as strongly attracted to the lean six-foot Canadian as he was to her but she kept him wondering. While she gave him smiles, she gave him no word of encouragement, and after spinning his visit out for as long as possible Hart finally had to go home without any certainty that he had won her. When he wrote she answered his letters, but it took another three-hundred-mile trip to Gloversville early in the new year before Eliza Ann (and, more reluctantly, her parents) accepted his suit.

Eager Hart was all for instant marriage but Eliza Ann had a trousseau to prepare. By June, 1847, she was ready, with a store of household linen made from cloth spun and woven by her mother, and kitchen utensils made by her farmer-tinsmith father. Her simple wedding dress of white dimity had long sleeves and a full gathered skirt, the neck outlined with fine cord. Her clothing was handmade, stitched with the same delicacy as the sampler she made when she was eight years old (now in the Winnipeg home of her great-granddaughter). She had been well trained in needlework, after the manner of the day. In pink and blue and brown thread (faded today) she had spent laborious hours stitching a little verse:

> The rose, the sweetly blooming rose,
> Ere from the tree 'tis torn,
> Is like the sweets that beauty shows
> In Life's exulting morn.

"I like to think," says her great-granddaughter, "that these few inches of cramped stitching, and that next section where the stitches slant a bit more than the rest, mark what she managed to get through at a sitting." Sewn into it is the story of a restless little girl's daily session with the needle, dutifully picked up and thankfully put down again to skip off to some childish activity after the enforced discipline of learning the proper accomplishments of a woman. But she may well have enjoyed creating the tiny embroidered houses with their sheltering trees, the birds that hung overhead in perpetual frozen flight and the beehives with their clouds of little brown bees. It would have been a proud moment when she put the last stitch to the last line: "Eliza Ann Phelps, Kingsboro, Montgomery Co., 1831."

Hart brought his bride home by canal boat and stage coach, probably introducing her proudly to the Watertown Masseys on the way, and ending the journey by steamboat from Sackett's Harbour, New York. At home, Daniel and Lucina awaited them. And Daniel—Daniel of the steel-trap jaw and the snapping eye, on the brink of a major change in his life—had written a little poem to welcome his new daughter-in-law.

Daniel by now had come to a momentous decision. For the past three years, while Hart worked on the farm in the summers and taught school in winter months, Daniel had spent all his time in his workshop, repairing his own farm implements and those of local farmers, learning the working details of the amazing new labour-saving devices that had begun to appear in the agricultural world. Without training, he taught himself by the practical application of everything he examined, not only repairing but actually making new parts for the machines. *Why not*, he began to think with growing excitement, *make the entire machine?*

For Daniel, when the opportunity occurred, to dream was to act. Near the tiny harbour of Bond Head, a mile south of Newcastle village in Durham County and nearly forty miles to the west of the Massey homestead, two small one-storey frame

24

buildings housing a foundry and blacksmith shop became available. In January, 1847, Daniel sold to Hart for the sum of £1,100, a hundred and eighty-five acres of his Grafton property, including the house and other buildings, and moved to Newcastle with Lucina and the remaining children, eighteen-year-old Eliza Jane, fifteen-year-old William Albert, Frances, twelve, and a four-year-old daughter, Arletta, who had been born in 1843. A tenth child, Alida, was born in Newcastle in November, 1847, and all the children lived to marry except William Albert, who in 1849 was to join the two little sisters and a brother already sorrowfully interred in the Academy Hill cemetery.

At first in partnership with the original owner, R. F. Vaughan (one of the promoters of the Bond Head Harbour development) and after a few months as sole owner, having bought out Vaughan, Daniel embarked on a new career at the age of forty-nine.

Today an orchard and market garden cover the site of Daniel's busy little plant, and the harbour of Bond Head, where schooners used to drop anchor right beside the flour mill, is reed-filled and quiet, lake water lapping the rotted piles of the retaining wall. But in 1847 all was bustle and industry. Daniel was successful from the start. In the first year only a few articles were made, simple ploughs and potash and sugar kettles. By 1848 harrows and cultivators had been added. By 1849 Daniel had more orders than he could fill.

In 1848 Daniel purchased about fifty acres of the east half of George Strange Boulton's property in the first concession in Newcastle (it had originally been a crown grant to King's College). The deed is dated March twenty-seventh, 1848, but actual possession of the land very likely took place when Daniel first moved to Newcastle a year earlier. Here he built a spacious cobblestone house with "peculiar dome and stately proportions," that was to become known in the family as "the old homestead." When his Bond Head business prospered so encouragingly, Daniel bought a solid two-storey brick factory building on the south side of the main Kingston Road, with another fifty acres of land, and moved his business early in 1849. With a six-horsepower engine, a machine shop with one lathe, a jigsaw and woodturning lathe in the workshop, a cupola furnace of one-ton capacity and ten employees, the "Newcastle Foundry And Machine Manufactory, C.W." (Upper Canada had become Canada West in 1841) moved bravely into the next phase of an enterprise that was to carry the Massey name to places as far apart as the Crimea in Russia and Wandiligong, Australia, and remain triumphantly world-wide down to the present day.

By 1851 the business—with a bigger horsepower engine and new machinery added to the plant—was too big for Daniel to handle alone. He asked Hart to join him, first as superintendent at a salary of four hundred dollars a year, and in 1852 as partner.

Since his father's departure from Grafton, Hart had been running a well organized farm and taking an active part in local affairs. He was appointed to the committee of the Agricultural Society of Northumberland in January, 1848, and was probably deeply involved in arrangements for the Provincial Grand Exhibition held in Cobourg in October that year.

When he left Grafton in answer to his father's request, Hart rented the property for a twelve-year term to a farmer named Groshaw, "117 acres more or less together with the houses, out houses, buildings, woods, ways, waters, water-courses, easements and appurtenances." For an annual rental of £57.10.0 Groshaw contracted to "conduct his operations of farming . . . in a proper husband-like manner . . . and seed down the said premises with clover and timothy every third crop and keep down all foul weeds such as Haddock stink weight [*sic*] and other noxious weeds . . . and pick up all loose stone upon the premises and pile the same either in heaps or against the fences . . ." Hart sold the property four years later and the lease was assigned to the new owner. He was twenty-eight in 1851 when he moved to the big white frame house next door to the Newcastle works with Eliza Ann, three-year-old Charles Albert (named for his mother's brother Charles and his father's dead brother William Albert) and Chester, one-year-old namesake of Eliza Ann's father in Gloversville.

Perhaps if Daniel alone had continued to control the business it might have developed only as a local success story (by 1854 the value of his real property was listed at £900, his taxable personal property at £100), but Hart's vigorous direction of policy, his tireless salesmanship, his almost uncanny sense of timing, were from the beginning aimed at targets beyond the horizon—though perhaps even Hart did not quite believe what he may have faintly envisaged. At this time he only knew that the sale of farm machinery was going well and could go better.

Against Daniel's cautious judgment, Hart obtained the rights to two American patents, and increased his implement line by Canadian-made Ketchum Mowers and Burrell Reapers (in 1855 replaced by the Manny Combined Hand-Rake Reaper and Mower). The origin of what was to become a mammoth world-wide enterprise lies less in the Masseys' personal inventiveness than in a shrewd assessment of Canadian production possibilities and the solid reputation the firm soon developed for excellence of workmanship. It would, in days to come, win prizes even against machines made in the United States by their own inventors. Not until some twenty years later did Massey-designed machinery appear.

Hart worked a sixty-hour week, occupied with multitudinous duties in the factory (his workday started at 7 A.M.) or travelling by horse and buggy through the district to attend field trials, demonstrations and agricultural exhibitions. With all this he still found time to be a school trustee and Bible-class leader. He was also a justice of the peace for Northumberland and Durham Counties and chief magistrate for a number of years.

Both Hart and his father were men of standing in the community though neither played any important part in politics, being content to give little more than moral support to the Reform Party. A gentleman reminiscing in *The Farm Implement News* in 1887 recalled that Daniel had been "a stanch reformer and supporter of the movement which McKenzie led." No doubt the Cobourg Conspiracy of 1839 was of disturbing interest to him. A July first meeting in Haldimand attended by about three hundred Reformers would very likely have included Daniel, and the excitement of events at the end of the month, when conspirators were landed from the American schooner *Guernsey* near Cobourg and subsequently tried and convicted after capture, would doubtless have been followed with deep concern. There is no record of his having taken an active part in the movement that led to the Rebellion of 1837. In later years Hart served as a member of the local branch of the Reform movement.

The Masseys were even then generous supporters of causes they believed in. The 1878 *Historical Atlas of Northumberland and Durham Counties* reported " . . . that [the Masseys] had found the congregation [of the Newcastle Methodist church] poor and neglected, and to their liberality the Methodists are indebted for the early completion [1847] of the church."

They were also men who despised inaction. A spirited exchange of letters in the *Cobourg Star* early in 1848 found Hart defending himself (with a fellow trustee) against accusations of high-handed action in the erection of a schoolhouse without proper authority. A tolerant and very logical letter appeared over both signatures (Charles Butler and Hart A. Massey) in the *Cobourg Star* of February ninth, together with a plan of the section. The question at issue was whether a new school should be erected to serve the children of nine lots and, if so, where. The new school had been built not quite in the centre of the section (on Lot 30 instead of Lot 31½) but, as the letter explained, more tax money and more pupils came from the favoured end. Butler had been replaced as trustee at the annual meeting by James

Craig who, the letter claimed, had been supported by the "United Irishmen" of the district.

We intend no reflection upon Mr. Craig and his countrymen, most of whom conduct themselves so well and so respectably in Canada, but the schoolroom was full of Irishmen, and it would be strange indeed if a meeting so constituted could by any possibility be quiet for five minutes together. We had an interlude of two or three coats being taken off for a fight, and before the business of the meeting was half gone through, there was a regular disturbance in the place.

A choleric reply from James Craig appeared on February twenty-third accusing Butler and Massey of an "endeavour to hold up the Irishmen residing in this School section . . . to the ridicule of your numerous readers." In the style of those days, the reply was peppered with italics and exclamation marks:

Is it not surprising that we have been thus long standing on the brink of a volcano, unaware of danger, until Providence revealed the awful fact to those sapient gentlemen, Messrs. Chas. Butler and Hart A. Massey?

It happens, unfortunately for *their* veracity, that the only disturbance which took place, was created by the elder Mr. Massey, *who endeavoured by that means, to prevent the resolutions condemnatory of his son and Mr. Butler being adopted by the meeting*, and during the interlude to which they refer, only *one* coat was pulled off, and that *not* by an Irishman, but by one of Mr. Butler's own countrymen, who was led into this outburst by the domineering spirit displayed by Mr. Massey, Sen'r and his party . . . Really, Mr. Editor, it is hard that your columns should be occupied with a subject so uninteresting to your readers as that of the squabbles attendant on a School meeting, but as Messrs. Butler and Massey thought proper to attack "Irishmen" in their letter, I consider it only due to myself and the other Irishmen who attended that School meeting, to publish this reply.

In the editorial columns of the same issue the *Star* commented tartly, "In another column will be found a letter from Mr. Craig respecting the schoolhouse referred to by Messrs. Massey and Butler. As each party has had his *say*, we hope that the matter will be allowed to drop."

In his home life Hart was happy. Together with a sunny temperament and an unexpected wit, Eliza Ann had brought to her marriage the sturdy thrift of her farm upbringing. As the wife of farmer Hart in the rambling house on the hill behind Cobourg, she had made the family supplies of soap and candles, cured hams and made sausages, baked bread and churned butter that took prizes at local fairs (she sold the extra butter at ten cents a pound) and cut and sewed clothing for Hart and the children.

"I thank the Lord," she told a friend, "that I had a mother who knew how to work and who taught me how to work." Many years later when the Massey women had servants to spare them from chores, poorer cousins in Cobourg heard with delight that Eliza Ann's daughter Lillian was expected to scrub the kitchen chairs.

In the Newcastle home Eliza Ann built a warm and loving refuge for busy Hart and the growing family. The year 1852 saw the birth and death of a baby boy, and 1854 brought the only daughter Lillian Frances. Eliza Ann read Bible stories to her small family from such books as *Line Upon Line* and *Peep of Day*. The children were close to their mother, and young faces would fall when, taking her part in community affairs, she had sometimes to be out.

"At times," a friend recalled, "when there were special calls for the heads of the house to be out in the evenings, as the shades of night had gathered the boys would say, 'Ma, are you going out this evening?' and when the answer was no, they would exclaim, 'Oh, I am so glad!' "

Charley, the eldest, was growing into a lively, restless youngster, with his mother's gentleness and his father's persistent interest in machines. He piled his blocks into shapes he called "threshing machines" and drove his mother distracted by disappearing into the plant next door to hang around the moving wheels. Once he was rescued just in time, as the end of his scarf brushed against the edge of a revolving shaft. Grandmother Lucina, knowing his fondness for dolls, made him a big rag doll to keep him from the machines. "Jinny" became his inseparable companion, carried under his arm in a way no girl would hold a doll, as he trotted along escorting to school a lady teacher who lived with the family, or went to visit his grandparents at the homestead only a few hundred yards from his own home.

Charley and small Chester loved to visit the old homestead. There were two young aunts to play with and to tease by pulling their dolls apart. Alida and Arletta were respectively only one and five years older than Charley. In later years he was not displeased to be mistaken for their brother when he visited them at college. Stern old Daniel, who retired from the business in 1855, had become an indulgent grandfather, tickled by the patently false innocence on the faces of his mischievous grandsons when they had hidden his tools. Lucina could be firmer and could threaten the slipper when they invaded her domain. Charley made himself useful bringing in wood and driving the cows to pasture, but these were chores undertaken for adventure and delight, never from the driving necessity that his father and grandfather had known.

At Christmas there would be a joyous family gathering at the homestead, with Charley and Chester marching noisily around the yard and the broad extensive verandas, blowing fife and banging drum. Every day at home there was the profitable business of gathering up the scrap-iron scattered around the yard and buildings. The children got one cent a pound for all they could collect, and their grandfather Phelps, on visits from Gloversville, would go around digging it up for the boys to find.

The world outside the small village was filled with stir and excitement. Charley was less than three weeks old when the first Provincial Grand Exhibition was held in Cobourg (when the judges had awarded his mother two special prizes of ten shillings and five shillings for quilts), but he was probably old enough, just after his seventh birthday, to visit the second one in 1855. All summer there was bustle and rush in Cobourg as buildings and tents went up inside the seven-foot board fence around what was now a twelve-acre fairground; cabbies and hotel keepers readied vehicles and rooms for the thousands of expected guests; steamships and schooners brought the exhibits by water, stagecoaches and carts trundled them in by land. Among the crowding visitors, Charley would cling close to his tall father, trying to ape his expressions of approval or criticism as they moved from the potted plants, fruits and vegetables in the Floral Hall to the sheaves of wheat, rolls and crocks of butter, and cheeses in the Dairy Produce, Grain and Seeds Hall. The ploughing match held on a nearby farm would be especially exciting, with (of course) father's machines performing best of all. He would not (though his father and grandfather might) be present at the grand dinner at the Globe Hotel attended by the Governor General, Sir Edmund Walker Head, and his lady, and some of the cabinet ministers from Toronto. But a little boy would never forget (if he were allowed to stay up so late) the firemen in their red flannel shirts and shiny black hats, led by the gleaming polished brass of the fire-engine as they formed a torchlight parade to escort the vice-regal party to the wharf at 11 P.M., and the flashing fireworks that rose into the night sky from the lighthouse. Perhaps the flamboyant Massey merchandising methods in later years, the pomp and circumstance of Delivery Day (when carloads of implements would be handed over to local agents with flags flying, bands playing and a parade), the jazzy four-colour catalogues and posters, all had their origin in Charles Massey's unforgettable boyhood discovery that everybody loves a good show.

Charley got his schooling first from a governess employed by Daniel for his younger children, then successively from the Academy, the common school and the grammar school in Newcastle. He had a particular talent for music. He could sight-read easily, and played the cabinet organ in the Newcastle

Methodist Church from the time he was thirteen. Later, when he was attending college in Cobourg, he had a harmonium in his room, and used to play the chapel organ for morning prayers.

These were days when the stimulation of progress was in the air. The Grand Trunk Railway from Montreal to Toronto was started in 1852 and each section, as completed, was opened with local celebrations. On a brilliant September Monday in 1856 an inaugural train with flag-bedecked engine ran over the section between Cobourg and Port Hope. It travelled at a breath-taking forty miles per hour for one part of the trip, and "could have maintained this speed all the way except for cows on the track." Since the Port Hope bridge had not been completed, the passengers walked through the town and boarded an awaiting train on the other side. The whole line was officially opened on October twenty-seventh, and Daniel, by invitation, rode proudly in the first train from Toronto to Montreal.

Less than a month later Daniel Massey died at the age of fifty-eight, staunchly refusing the liquor that was prescribed to stimulate him, "the most tender-hearted man," said Hart, "that ever breathed."

Daniel died intestate, and the property was divided between his son Hart and his two young daughters Arletta and Alida (thirteen and nine), "reserving all rights of the Relict of said Daniel Massey deceased." The homestead lot went to the two girls, who lived there with their mother until Lucina died in the 1860s. Then, aged twenty-four and twenty, they sold all their inheritance to Hart.

Daniel had died just before the tenth anniversary of the purchase of his small foundry but he had lived to see its output quadrupled (the company would repeat this in every following decade). The Grand Trunk extended the company's market. Indeed, toward the end of 1856 Hart sent a carload of machines to the Provincial Exhibition at Kingston and won the first of

33

Kinsale Association
Library.

thousands of medals and awards that would come to Massey-made equipment in succeeding years. (More than a hundred years later, in October, 1965, a Finnish farmer drove a Massey-Ferguson tractor to win the world ploughing contest at Oslo, Norway).

Newspapers of the day, for today's readers, are sadly lacking in local and human-interest news, since local gossip circulated quickly by word of mouth through tea meetings, quilting bees, barn raisings, agricultural shows, church services and the other social congregations of the district. The columns of the press were filled instead with "cultural" material: poems, letters, stories calculated to uplift the moral tone of the neighbourhood, fierce political arguments, news from abroad for the news-hungry immigrants still tied by nostalgia to their native lands. The doings of Westminster were often reported more excitedly and in far greater detail than those in Toronto. Hearts in Cobourg were as lightened by the relief of Lucknow as those anywhere in the world, and as stirred by the news that "Dr. Livingstone has this week sailed for Lisbon and . . . intends to return for a short time to England before finally starting for the scene of his scientific and missionary labours."

Yet, of course, local events were important. In January, 1858, everyone was looking forward to Canadian decimal coinage and interested in the decision, as "safe and central," that Ottawa was to be the seat of government. Citizens complained about the wooden sidewalks (they remained in use until almost 1900) and the danger of stepping on loose boards that would often fly up, bringing a protest from one gentleman that this had caused his companion to "lose her perpendicular."

The *Cobourg Star* was concerned about the effects of modern life on the younger generation. "We cannot . . . avoid the remark that, highly delighted as we were with the *singing* [at the Floral Concert], we had serious misgivings as to the effects which such a dramatically disposed entertainment would have

34

on the minds of children; and considering that they were a body of Sunday School children belonging to a Church strongly averse to anything like theatrical amusements, we more than doubt the propriety of any such exhibition." And in an early issue of the newly published Newcastle *Recorder* appeared the sad and cautionary tale of two young ladies who daringly drove around the Mountain in Montreal with their bonnets attached to the backs of their heads. The cold wind got to their brains: one died almost immediately after returning from the drive, the other went insane first and then died. "It is high time," said the *Recorder* severely, "for fathers of families to interfere and insist upon the abolishment of an attire so very dangerous, so very unbecoming, and so much despised by the male portion of the community."

By 1857 the Newcastle plant had been enlarged by the addition of a thirty-horsepower engine, new engine lathes, planers, turning lathes. The *Recorder* carried an advertisement headed "Encourage Home Manufactures," in which Hart stated his readiness to manufacture at short notice a large variety of implements: "steam engines of any description, steam dredges and boilers, brass and iron castings and forgings, engine lathes and turning lathes, iron and wood planes and other kinds of machinery required in an Engine Shop, Carriage Manufactory, or other establishment of a similar kind." Confidently extolling the Ketchum, Manny and Burrell machines, other implements and "nine varieties of plows," Hart continued, "The Subscriber flatters himself that with his superior facilities he can compete with any establishment of a similar kind in Canada or the United States."

By 1861 the enlarged plant employed about fifty men in the pre-harvest rush. Hart dropped some of the smaller utensils from his list and added Wood's Mower by agreement with its American inventor. In 1862 the first Massey catalogue was issued for what was now known as The Newcastle Agricultural

Works—twenty-eight pages of glowing description and terms, with line drawings of the implements offered, inside a dark blue cover lettered in gold and carrying an illustration of the medal won at the Prince of Wales Exhibition, Montreal. A year later, the introduction of Wood's Self-Rake Reaper flooded the firm with more orders than Hart could comfortably fill.

At the end of March, 1864, when young Charley (now a tall boy of sixteen) was in the first of his two years at Victoria College in Cobourg, the Massey works were destroyed by fire, taking with them all completed orders, all the partly constructed implements and all the plant's machinery and equipment except a few patterns. The loss was estimated at about $25,000. Though somewhat harassed by domestic affairs (Eliza Ann gave birth five days later to their fifth child, Walter Edward Hart), Hart Massey was too resilient to be stopped by such a blow. A year's business was lost while new plant and machinery were acquired, but he was back on his feet in 1865 with sales of more than four hundred implements and more orders, again, than he could fill.

These were times when the world was astir with alternately "horrid" and wondrous events. The people of the Canadian backwoods followed with painful eagerness the proclamations signed A. Lincoln, and the front-line despatches from Bull Run and Atlanta and Gettysburg. On April twenty-second, 1865, the weathered farmers, the busy tradesmen and the gentry of Northumberland and Durham Counties read with appalled fascination that the President of the United States had been "foully murdered" just over a week earlier. They shook their heads over the macabre details and rumours that followed the dreadful deed: that the assassin had himself been killed two weeks later; that Barnum (of circus fame) had offered a thousand dollars to buy the pillow on which Lincoln had died, and an unnamed but immense sum for the boots worn by John Wilkes Booth; that four men had been killed in New

Orleans and six in Nashville, Tennessee, for publicly rejoicing at the President's death. They marvelled at the courage with which he had ignored the death threats found in a package in his desk, labelled "assassination letters" in his own hand.

On a note very familiar today, the *Cobourg Sentinel* was deploring the drain of emigrants to the United States "by thousands a week." This was not, the *Sentinel* said, because Canada afforded no field for enterprise and no recompense for diligent labour, nor because the emigrants generally found fault with the government or the country's internal organization. But nearly a hundred thousand Canadians had entered the Northern Army because, the *Sentinel* said, the government had concentrated on abstract ideas instead of building roads, widening canals, and giving assistance to settlers in the back townships.

The Young Manager

In 1866 young Charley Massey left college and spent a few weeks as a Massey workman, running a lathe in the iron-finishing department. That fall, with his brother Chester, sixteen, his sister Lillian, twelve, and his two aunts Arletta and Alida, now twenty-three and nineteen, Charles went off on a memorable tour of the western United States, visiting Kalamazoo, Chicago, Dubuque and Cleveland. For the five young Canadians, used to quiet village life, this was a gala holiday, their visit the occasion for festive gatherings at the homes of relatives and friends.

In Kalamazoo they were welcomed at the home of a pioneer citizen, Hiram Arnold, whose wife, Betsey Woodbury Massey, was a second cousin of Hart. Her father, Edward Massey, a younger brother of immigrant Daniel, had died when she was a child, and she had been brought up in the home of an older cousin, Solon Massey, in Watertown. Her husband, Hiram Arnold, had come to Kalamazoo as a young man from New York State after saving one thousand dollars from his earnings as a clerk in the mercantile lumber business. With his thousand dollars he bought the goods salvaged from a vessel wrecked at the mouth of the Kalamazoo river *en route* to New Buffalo, and opened a store in Kalamazoo. In 1842, a time of money scarcity, he began shipping wheat east on behalf of local farmers, moved into the produce business, and from there to banking. In 1859 he had purchased a farm on the old plank road about two miles north of the town, where he planted an orchard and "grapery" and built a gracious gabled house as a summer residence.

The Arnolds loved to entertain. "His home was the scene of the most enjoyable social events in the then village," said the *Kalamazoo Gazette* when Hiram died in July, 1892, at the age of eighty-four. "He was the friend of young people and enjoyed their company and was never so happy as when in their midst. Many is the brilliant party that was held at the residence of Hiram Arnold in pioneer days."

Parties and sightseeing kept the five young Masseys and the six young Arnolds busy during the visit. Twenty-seven-year-old cousin Delevan was an especially romantic figure, just back from two years in Detroit and a veteran of the recent Civil War. He had been a good correspondent while he was away (his lengthy letters home covering the first year of his experiences were published in a booklet by the Kalamazoo Public Museum a hundred years later) and could hold his Canadian cousins spellbound with the exciting stories of his recent adventures. "Our two companys went out scouting to see where the Rebels were," he would tell his enthralled audience. "I was ahead of the column with five men as advance guard passing through the mountains; we saw three of them on the road and gave chase. They turned a bend in the road at the foot of a hill and were out of sight. But as we came around the hill, there they were within five rods of us with their rifles levelled, and as we came in sight, fired. One missed his aim, but that of the others was deadly, two of the men, from Company H, reeled in their saddles and fell dead. The scoundrels wheeled their horses and fled amid a shower of pistol bullets, unharmed. They had very good horses, and before we could hardly think they had made their escape."

He would tell about being taken prisoner and afterwards exchanged, and how in another battle his horse was shot from under him, falling on him and causing injuries that won him an honourable discharge in August, 1864; how he saw the statue of "Freedom" that was to adorn the top of the dome of the Capitol in Washington when it was completed, "a splendid thing, twenty feet high, and of bronze." He would recall his visit to Mount Vernon, where he "took a good look at the home of Washington . . . It looks much like all the homes of the wealthy Virginia planters, and is going to decay fast." Perhaps he would bring out the souvenirs of his visit, several pieces of wood from the Mount Vernon house, and the rose geranium leaf he picked from the grave of the "Father of His Country." (Would it be pressed in the family Bible?)

But the letters, written from the cold and muddy camps outside Washington and Charleston and Columbus, where the rain fell in torrents and the wind blew more than half of the tents over, were threaded with the aching homesickness of a boy from a loving family environment:

You must have such pleasant evenings around that great fireplace, with those noisy children thrashing about and carrying on . . . I should like to be there and dance at one of those parties but I don't suppose that I should make a very good appearance in the presence of ladies, for I have not even had a chance to speak to one since I left Michigan . . . How dearly I should love to be home this spring, to help fit up "Brookside" for the summer campaign . . . I am so glad you have got a girl that can take the work off your hands. You, my dear mother, have worked enough to be waited on the rest of your life, and may that be a long one . . . I received a good long letter . . . from Jessie which gave me great pleasure. She writes a very good letter, and a very good hand for so young a girl . . .

Pretty, winsome Jessie, who was only nine when her big brother was away at the front, at thirteen had developed a charm and sparkle that her cousin Charley did not forget.

On the way home the young travellers spent a day visiting the Provincial Fair held that year in Toronto, where the honour of representing Canadian manufacturing at next year's International Exposition in Paris, France, had been awarded by a government committee to Massey harvesting machinery. Then the little party separated, Arletta and Alida returning to the Wesleyan Female College in Hamilton, the other three to their home in Newcastle. But Charles was back in Toronto in a couple of weeks for a year of further study, first at the British-American Commercial College at the corner of King and Toronto Streets, and then at the Military College. At the Commercial College he had received a "Thorough Practical Business Education that covered Mining, Milling, Manufacturing, Commission, Foreign Exchange, Steamboating, Railroading, Banking, Commercial Law, Commercial Arithmetic, Letter writing, etc., Telegraphy and Phonography Extra." By 1867 nineteen-year-old Charles was ready to enter the firm as his father's right hand.

The year 1867 has achieved historical distinction as the year of Confederation in Canada. The *Cobourg Sentinel* marked it with the publication of the proclamation issued by Queen Victoria on May twenty-fourth setting July first as the date for the union of the provinces of Upper and Lower Canada, Nova Scotia and New Brunswick, to be the Dominion of Canada. In the following month, the *Sentinel* published a timely editorial urging the adoption of a new banner for the new Dominion:

Its adoption by Parliament would of course be necessary and it is unfortunate that the design could not be decided upon [so] that the new ensign could be unfurled to the breeze on the joyful holiday approaching, when the Dominion will become a fact, and the Provinces enter upon a new and glorious era. Our new Dominion should certainly have a national flag, and that flag should have upon it, as an emblem of the industry, skill and perseverance of our people, the Canadian Beaver, and as an emblem of our permanence and stability, a leaf or branch of our Canadian Maple, whose hardy nature has ever nobly and unharmed stood the blasts and severity of our Canadian winters. We all love that time-honoured banner, which, "for a thousand years," etc. etc., and we still claim that as our flag, as Britons; but while we do so, we want an emblem also to distinguish us as Canadians. We vote for a National Banner for the Dominion of Canada.

The banner was to be longer delayed than they knew but the celebrations on the first Dominion Day were cheerful. In Cobourg the bells rang out shortly after midnight, and the day was punctuated by frequent discharge of cannon and small arms. At noon, five volunteer companies (including Grafton) gathered on the common, where a *feu de joie* was fired by the artillery, with cheers for Queen and new Dominion. A torchlight procession and brilliant fireworks completed the day.

In the Massey family the year 1867 had other reasons for importance. May twenty-fourth brought to Hart and Eliza Ann their sixth and last child, Frederic Victor (named for the birthday of the Queen). In the fall Hart went to Europe to supervise his exhibits at the Paris Exposition, where Massey-made Woods machines were awarded the Imperial Cross of the Legion of Honour by the Emperor of France. Hart was away from home for two months and young Charles was left in charge of a business that now employed a hundred men and made its sales through more than twenty agencies across the new Province of Ontario.

In Charles Albert Massey all the qualities of his father and grandfather came to full flower, with something added. Daniel had the shrewdness and courage, Hart the foresight and aggressiveness; Charles added charm and a strong sense of showmanship. Though the escapades of his youth were boylike enough, a business friend would say later, "Charles never was a boy; he was always a man," perhaps because most of his spare time was spent hanging around the works rather than out playing with his schoolboy friends. He had mastered the intricacies of machinery through his inquisitive interest in them almost from babyhood, and added to this a sound study of business methods. It was probably Charles who shipped an 1868 order of twenty mowers and reapers to Germany in boxcars hung with red, white and blue bunting, daubed with information about their freight load and dispatched with music from the town band and the cheers of Newcastle villagers.

Though the order from Germany and the purchase of a mower by the Emperor Napoleon III after the Paris Exposition field trials may have given Hart a fleeting vision of an export market for Massey machines, this was looking too far into the future. With Charles' enthusiastic co-operation, he set about widening the scope of national sales.

But those early days of hard-driving work were beginning to tell on Hart. More and more he delegated responsibility to Charles. In the summer of 1868 he took Eliza Ann and the four younger children for an extended trip to the seashore, leaving Charles in full charge of the factory.

Then in 1870, at forty-seven, Hart took the advice of his doctor and decided to involve himself in something less exacting. The firm was formed into a joint stock company (capital stock was a hundred thousand dollars) as the Massey Manufacturing Company, with Hart as nominal president and Charles as vice-president and superintendent.

That done, Hart made plans to move to Cleveland, Ohio, where he had numerous friends and family connections. He took his family to stay in the old homestead, while Charles, who had never forgotten the girl he met in Kalamazoo in 1866, completely renovated and refurnished the frame house next door to the works. On October twelfth, 1870, Charles crossed the border to marry seventeen-year-old Jessie Fremont Arnold in a simple ceremony at Brookside, the home of her merchant-banker father outside Kalamazoo, where the visitors from Canada had been entertained so royally four years earlier. He brought his bride back to Newcastle after a wedding trip to Detroit and Cleveland, where the young couple visited the many Massey relatives. Ten years earlier, Jessie's brother Delevan had stopped off in Cleveland on the first day of his journey to the war, and his cousins Albert and Will Massey had come on board the boat for a half-hour visit. (Only a week later, twenty-two-year-old Will had joined up, too, to die of wounds in April, 1863.)

The following year when their new home in Cleveland was ready, Hart and Eliza Ann moved in, taking with them Chester, now twenty-one, seventeen-year-old Lillian, and the two younger children, Walter, seven, and four-year-old Fred Victor. Early in 1872 Hart sold the old Newcastle homestead to the Reverend Henry Brent and his wife Sophia; the building still stands, though the cobblestone exterior has been refaced with brick. It has been used as the Anglican rectory in Newcastle since its purchase for that purpose in 1896.

Hart, as president and director of the Empire Coal Company in Cleveland, found plenty to keep him busy without the strain and physical energy he had expended on what was now the Massey Manufacturing Company, though he kept in close touch with the latter. What he had left was simply another successful and quite promising local industry, and it seems probable that Hart went to Cleveland with no realization of the giant it would become, happy only in the thought that he had provided his son with a good living. It was due to the management of his son, Charles Albert Massey, that the company flourished, grew, and finally burst beyond the boundaries of a small Ontario village.

Charles, now twenty-three, taller than his six-foot father, with a fine head and large clear eyes, "stood at the helm of affairs like an old veteran." All his training and inclination had been directed to this end. The company steadily prospered, Charles enlarged and improved the works, and was compensated for the long hours in the office by the proximity of his young bride in the white frame house right next door.

In October, 1871, their first child, Eugene Arnold, was born and died after living for only one day. When Jessie was strong enough Charles took her for a trip across the border to visit his family in Cleveland and hers in Kalamazoo. In the following November he was able to report the birth of a daughter who, after a discussion by letter of suitable names, was christened Winona Grace ("Winnifred is not a favorite name with us," Hart answered his son's query in a letter dated December fourth, 1872. "Winona Grace is much prettyer.") The baby's five-year-old uncle Fred was particularly excited. Charles had covered his pride by a teasing comment that the new baby was probably not worth much more than fifty cents. "Your mother was reading your letter to Fred," reported Hart in his sprawling writing, "and when she came to that part about selling the babe for fifty cents, he says 'What, sell the babe for fifty cents, I would give that for it,' and wanted me to sit write down and write you his offer as he has got just that amount, so that if it is still in the market you can make out the papers and the money will be forthcoming." (Hart's spelling in his business letters was much more precise.)

They planned an early visit to see their first grandchild. "Our present arrangements are to leave here on Thursday after New Year's day go to the Bridge that night remain there till morning arrive in Toronto at 11 A.M. remain there till evening and down to N that night. Walter and Fred will accompany us. Your mother," Hart continued, "has a bad cold just now and added to it by going down to the City today but I hope it may not last long."

Hard-headed in business and growing more autocratic year by year, Hart was always devoted to Eliza Ann. Though he was "not richly endowed with the lighter surface qualities that make men popular"—the verdict of a contemporary—"yet he was capable of deep tenderness and affection, and those who knew him well enough to love him, loved him well." Even in the business world there were those who found him "a great favorite, and in private and social life he has many warm and attached friends."

Rugged, angular and inflexible were adjectives often applied to his character, but within the bosom of his family he was affectionate, with a dry sense of humour. He was obviously in tune with gentler Charles, whose religious attitudes, less stern and narrowly defined than his father's, were sincere enough to satisfy that demanding moralist. Cleveland was not far enough away to break the ties that bound them and, besides, the firm was still in the forefront of Hart's mind. The exchange of letters and family visits continued.

Other letters went out to the United States from the small Ontario village. The little Kalamazoo girl who wrote "a very good letter" to her soldier brother in the early 1860s kept her mother closely in touch with the daily life of her "loving child Jessie." The summer of 1873 was a hard one for the young bride. Seven-months-old Winnie was teething, and Charley's mother, on a visit to Newcastle, had fallen seriously ill. Jessie wrote in June:

I have just got Winnie settled in the cradle. She has been having a hard crying spell. Yesterday and today she has cried about half the time and I don't know what ails her . . . I feel just tired out myself. Mrs. Massey keeps just about the same, no improvement since I wrote last. I forgot to tell you that Mr. M. bought a cow. I am glad he did for buying milk was a nuisance, he also bought us a barrell of sugar and chest of tea, so you see he is quite generous . . . I am about discouraged about Mrs. Massey. I don't believe she will get up this summer, and think of the family we have and then no prospect of its being smaller. I wish they had staid at home in the spring and then she would have been there now. Of course they try and make as little trouble as possible but they must make some.

Life in the backwoods village had distinct drawbacks:

I am sick of cold backward Canada, living on meat and potatoes half the time isn't very nice. I am in an awful hurry for peas, but must wait some time yet. I have had an awful time trying to get Winnie something to wear on her head and at last had to make her one and that looks like a fright but I guess she will have to wait till she is larger. They don't have anything here for babies to wear.

Even culture came accompanied by discomfort. "There is to be a concert in the Drill shed tonight," Jessie wrote. "Miss Grace Edgerton is the singer. Charley wants me to go, but I am afraid the shed will be too damp. There was a rain last night, and it will be wet in there with no floor."

But there were compensations. She was free of her in-laws by October: "We received a card from Lilly today saying her Mother was getting much better, as she could walk into cousin Albert's room," and Charley gave her what luxuries he could. For a while

46

there was a girl to help in the house but Nellie proved to be more trouble than she was worth. "I had extra work in the shape of a large Turkey to stuff and get ready for dinner. Of course Nellie isn't the least help about any such thing. It takes all her time to wash dishes and sweep up the rooms out there." With no visitors to cope with, Jessie wrote that she was feeling quite well, "and do not think the care of Winnie will hurt me any, not any more than the bother with Nellie did."

If baby clothes were hard to come by, the district could supply garments for ladies that were quite acceptable:

Charley went to Bowmanville yesterday, I sent by him to bring me home some kind of a cloak, so he brought me one trimmed with white fox fur, very pretty indeed. There is also a great deal of jet trimming on it. The sleeves have large cuffs edged with the fur. It is tight fitting in the back. The retail price is $25, they brought it from Toronto for a pattern cloak. I think I shall keep it as I shall not be likely to suit myself better, it fits me so nicely.

The proximity of the house to the factory meant that the young father could run in and out at odd moments of the day. "The whistle has just blown for noon, and I must go and look at my Turkey," Jessie wrote. "Charley plays with [the baby] so much, she cries for him now when he goes out and wants to stay with him all the time he is in the house."

The years from 1871, when Charles took over management of the Massey firm, to 1879, when the company finally outgrew its village home, were years of proud achievement for him. In the first five years under the young manager's leadership business increased 50 per cent. Alert to progress, receptive of new ideas, young Charles seized every opportunity that came his way and sought out others for himself. The big chimneys poured smoke year-round, since there were always enough orders unfilled at the season's end to keep the men employed through the winter.

Hart's frequent visits and advice were welcome but Charles had confidence in his own judgment. In 1874 a new Sulky Horse

Kinsale Association
Library

Rake invented by an American named Sharp so impressed him
that he obtained the rights for Canadian manufacture, eventually buying the patent rights for Ontario, Quebec and the new
Province of Manitoba. The four-colour catalogues waxed ecstatic
in the by-now-usual Massey way, full of testimonials from satisfied
users and announcements of awards piled up over the years. ("A
boy six years old, with a pony, raked forty-five acres of hay and
about thirty acres of stubble, and the little fellow feels proud of
his pony and Sulky Rake," stated one P. W. Whelihan, of
Thornhill Place.) The slogan "No Equal or No Sale" was
rammed home in copy and in cartoon. The twelve-page 1870
catalogue proudly claimed that the Massey Manufacturing
Company had no old stock to offer at reduced prices because the
factory could never keep up with the demand.

Charles had always believed strongly in the power of advertising. In 1875 a four-page paper, the *Massey Pictorial*, had made the
first of several irregular appearances. One leaflet was illustrated
with the prize medals won by Massey-made machines, including
a first-prize medal from Sydney, Australia.

By 1877 the works had increased to ten buildings (one had
three storeys, another two) and a sixty-horsepower engine had
been installed. The catalogue promised from two to three thousand Sharp's Rakes for the harvest of 1878. The Massey Harvester, added to the list in 1878 and the first truly Canadian
design, was an instant success. An expected two hundred orders
had been more than doubled, and the works, even on day-
and-night shifts, were able to fill only three hundred and fifty-six
of the five hundred orders.

In 1878 it was apparent that the business had outgrown its
original home. In 1876 Charles Massey had submitted a brief at
the invitation of the House of Commons Select Committee on the
Causes of the Depression in Trade and Commerce, and reported
a gross of a hundred thousand dollars. The thirty-two-page
catalogue of 1879 carried an insert, dated September first, 1879,
announcing the company's imminent removal to Toronto.

48

Though the protective tariff introduced by Sir John A. Macdonald in 1878 was raised from 17½ per cent to 25 per cent (raised again in 1883 to 35 per cent), Charles Massey was against the increase. ". . . The existing *tariff* is satisfactory to us, and is sufficient protection," he had stated in his 1876 brief, "perhaps even a little less would also be. A still further advance in the tariff would certainly prove adverse to our interest." Its effects reached into his home as well as his business. Dutiful Jessie wrote to her "dear mother":

We have just completed seven pairs of drawers for Winnie, and they are all very pretty. I got my cotton over just in time as there is now a great deal higher duty on everything since the National Policy came into force, and they will now be much more strict. Charley's circulars which are coming from Buffalo will be $400.00 more than expected on account of the raised duties. Perhaps you don't read Canadian affairs enough to know why this is. I believe it is to protect the Manufacturers in Canada.

In Cleveland, Hart had been occupied with what had become the Cleveland Coal Company in 1877. The family had lived in the Ohio city for ten years, first at 1110 Wilson Avenue, later at 753 Euclid Avenue. Chester and Lillian were young adults who lived the pleasant and relaxed social life of many holiday trips and family visits. Chester was for a time an agent for the Provident Life and Trust Company. All of them were deeply involved in the work of the Methodist Church. The younger boys, Walter and Fred Victor, first attended public school and were later enrolled in Brooks School in the new building erected in 1875, a year after its establishment, Walter in the academic department, Fred in the preparatory department. The school building, which was burned down in 1908, was "of Anglo-Swiss architecture, beamed on the outside and painted in chocolate and vermilion upon the projecting portions over a drab groundwork." It had a gymnasium and a chemical laboratory and, equipped with a drill hall and armoury, provided military training. The school's scholastic standards were high, and Walter's averages were good enough (67.8 and 73.7 per cent in two succeeding years) to win him a place on the Roll of Merit.

Hart had been happy in Cleveland. But now, suddenly aware of what Charley had done for the Massey Manufacturing Company, he made immediate plans to return to Canada and become active president once more. While Chester and Lillian (now twenty-eight and twenty-four) were away on a European trip, Hart and Eliza Ann brought the two younger boys to Newcastle for the summer of 1878, when father and son pored over their plans for next year's big move and sat long into the night discussing details and costs and the daring imaginative innovations they hoped to introduce.

As early as March that year Jessie had written to her mother, "We shall not take up any carpets this spring, as the prospect for our going away is so favorable: they are now making the plans for the buildings. The people are beginning to realize in a sleepy way that we really mean to go." All through the summer of 1879 Charles commuted between Newcastle and Toronto, supervising the building of the massive plant at the western edge of the provincial capital. The site of the new plant was a six-acre triangular section on King Street known as the Old Exhibition Grounds, immediately behind the Queen Street Lunatic Asylum.

The new Toronto factory created a stir not only throughout Canada but across the border. With the main railway tracks on one side of the six-acre site (private spur lines ran into the works) and the horse-drawn streetcar line on the other, the huge three-storey-and-basement main building of solid red brick presented an imposing appearance. All the buildings were lit by gas and safeguarded from fire by an automatic sprinkler system. It was the Masseys' ambition to produce everything needed in the manufacture of farm machinery, even the tools with which it was made. The orderly system by which materials moved through the plant was not unlike modern production-line methods. It was obvious that advantage had been taken of the most up-to-date techniques.

50

At the end of 1879 Charles and Jessie moved into their new home at 1 Clarence Square on the corner of Spadina Avenue, a dozen blocks to the east of the works. From the corner house of a red brick row with a charming view over the lake (now blocked by factories, bridges and reclaimed land), Charles could drive easily to and from the office along tree-lined dirt roads. It was not too far, indeed, to walk on good days, past the old garrison church of St. John's and the military cemetery where the dead of 1812 were buried. Clarence Square still stands, green and tree-shaded, but the large fountain in the centre is gone, and a gas station occupies the site of Charles Massey's first Toronto home, where he and Jessie set up housekeeping with Winnie, now seven, five-year-old Arthur Lyman and four-year-old Jennie Louise. In August, 1880, a second son, Charles Albert, was born; a year later Bessie Irene completed the little family.

Hart's sojourn in Cleveland was nearing an end. The family had spent eleven happy years in that city, where its head had become a man of consequence. "They are getting up a new street railroad between the City and Newbury," he had written to Charles only a year after his arrival, "and I was solicited by the leading parties to take the presidency and manage the road. But I think I shall decline."

Hart's real love had always been the firm he had helped to develop from a small blacksmith's shop on a country road. At the end of 1882, now that it had become a mighty monster on Toronto's King Street West, Hart Massey at fifty-nine came back to Canada to take control of the family business once again.

Hart's return to Toronto in the fall of 1882 almost proved fatal. He had bought from A. R. McMaster (not the senator) a twenty-five-room mansion, a Victorian period piece all gables and turrets, pseudo-Tudor chimneys, porches and bay windows, on fashionable, tree-lined Jarvis Street, and was preparing to move in when he was stricken with what four doctors pronounced a mortal illness. To his eldest son, who urgently needed his father's active help and presence, this was a disaster.

His real rapport with his father made it also a great personal shock. The family gathered round in anxious sorrow, and (in the hyperbole of the day) "the filial affection and watchful anxiety of noble Charles were beautiful to notice." Fortunately all their fears proved baseless. Tough, grey-bearded Hart rallied, recovered, and was soon throwing his restless energy into the business, which for the next few years kept the chimneys belching, the buildings expanding and the staff working at top pitch.

As early as 1876 the Masseys owned patent rights for a machine invented by one of their Newcastle employees, an automatic binder to tie the sheaves with twine. Experimental work on a wire-binder went as far as an actual model in 1879, which proved unsatisfactory. When in 1881, far-sighted Charles initiated the purchase of a competitor, the Toronto Reaper and Mower Company, the Masseys acquired a practical light twine-binder. After work had been done to simplify the implement (which the Toronto company had also been manufacturing under American licence), a hundred farmers were chosen to test the models in the harvest of 1882. It was the enthusiastic response to this machine that had brought Hart permanently to Toronto again. It doubled the output of the Massey plant: by 1883 the Massey Manufacturing Company's aggregate business was a million dollars, more than ten times the amount done in 1870, the year of its incorporation.

Hart and Eliza Ann were delighted to be back in Canada and able to enjoy frequent visits with their five active young grandchildren. Charles and Jessie had made a happy home in Clarence Square, where Charles romped each night with the children as he had in earlier days with his baby brother Fred Victor. (Once he had nursed Fred lovingly through a childhood illness in Newcastle when the rest of the family were away.) Shortly after coming to Toronto, he and Jessie had joined the congregation of Metropolitan Church on Queen Street East, "the Cathedral of

Methodism in Ontario," built just over ten years earlier. In December, 1882, with Hart, Eliza Ann and the four young Masseys beside them at the communion rail, Charles and Jessie were received into the church in a moving ceremony that had been postponed because of Hart's illness. If Charley's attendance was somewhat sketchy, the distance from Clarence Square was accepted as an adequate reason: his genuine interest in religious affairs was never in question.

Charles had been working at the top of his capacity, engaging staff, adjusting wages, planning the vigorous advertising, making business trips that took him reluctantly away from Jessie and the children, superintending sales, banking and the numerous agencies throughout the country (the first one in the new Province of Manitoba had been established in 1881). He had been writing, by hand, as many as a hundred and fifty letters a day. Though he had served for a year in Newcastle as a councillor, he found himself too busy in Toronto to accept an invitation to stand for election to the Dominion Parliament. Now, with Hart back in charge, he was able to delegate some of the burden. And none too soon: even Charley's robust health was beginning to show signs of strain.

But though the work was now shared, Charley's exuberant interest in everything would never allow him an unoccupied moment. As a student at Victoria College in Cobourg he had been an interested member (for a time one of the board of directors) of the Literary Association. "I ought to spend two hours each day reading," he complained to Jessie. "I'd go to college now, if only I had the time." In Newcastle in 1875 he had started a small four-page paper, the *Massey Pictorial*, brightly reporting the firm's advance and growth. In 1881 he started a monthly publication, *Massey's Illustrated* (which was to reach a circulation of seventy thousand in later years), announcing the opening of the new Toronto plant. His enthusiasm for music—two of his father's wedding presents had been a harmonium and a piano—

had spurred the employees to start the Massey Cornet Band in 1881. With his father on the scene again, the business booming, a pretty wife and five beautiful children, the future belonged to Charles Massey.

After the 1883 summer rush was over, Charles and Jessie decided to combine pleasure with business and take a three-week trip to Manitoba, visiting Chicago and St. Paul on the way and dropping in on Jessie's family at Kalamazoo. The Massey name had created some awe on the prairies; in the small parlour of their Brandon hotel a woman gushed, "Is this the great Mr. Massey who sends us the wonderful machines?" Charles acknowledged his identity with suitable solemnity but he and Jessie chuckled over the incident in the privacy of their room. His heady success in business never robbed Charles of an endearing humility.

Though the travellers were delayed for three days in Winnipeg when Charles developed acute indigestion, they were eager to be home again. Back in Toronto big things were afoot. The factory and foundry were being extended again, doubling the 1879 working space, to turn out machines with resounding names like *The King of the Meadows*, *The Queen of the Harvesters*, *The Mighty Monarch of the Harvest Field*. A new office building, which was to contain a reading room, library and lecture hall for the workmen, was one of Charley's most absorbing projects. And even more exciting, a fine new house on Jarvis Street, little more than a hundred yards from the Massey mansion and built on a lot owned by the Honourable Edward Blake (leader of the Liberal opposition in Ottawa, and a family friend) was being prepared, better suited to the needs of a growing family and the increasing prestige of a Massey vice-president. They moved in November, entranced by the new neighbourhood with its nearness to their church and good schools for the children.

At Christmas that year Hart had reason to feel a deep pride and satisfaction in the family that gathered joyously at 433 Jarvis Street (it was later renumbered 515): Chester, now thirty-three

54

and at six-foot-three the tallest of his sons; fair-haired Lillian, twenty-nine and the apple of his eye; Walter, nineteen, home for the holidays from his first term at Massachusetts Institute of Technology in Boston and bubbling about a very special Boston girl; the sixteen-year-old kid brother, Fred Victor, showing off the latest product of his workbench; and Charles—Charles of the winning personality, with his lovely wife and charming children. At family prayers that night, with the servants called in from the kitchen, Hart offered special thanks to heaven for his good fortune.

Not two months later, on February twelfth, 1884, Charles Massey was dead of typhoid fever. He was thirty-five.

They had tried everything. A blood transfusion proved useless ("Poor Minnie," Charles whispered as the donor left the room, "she has suffered so much to save my life"); so did a desperate, experimental injection of milk into the veins. Wrung with sorrow, Hart exclaimed, "I would rather go than see you go, Charley." After directing his three older children to Bible study and Sunday school attendance, Charles said weakly, "I want to see my babies." Solemn-eyed, Bertie and Bessie were brought in to kiss their father goodbye. Throughout his intense suffering Charles urged his family and attendants to go out for fresh air, and remembered to send a message to Walter who, back at MIT, could not return to Toronto in time to see his brother alive.

Sorrowfully, Hart completed the office building at the works and put up a stained glass window as a tribute to his oldest son, "the beloved vice-president and manager, whose portrait, a refined and gentle face, has below it a Perfect Binder, standing in a field of ripened grain, a beautiful simile of this worker's life." In the home Jessie and Charles had occupied so briefly, the young widow tried to make plans for the future. Small Bertie, seeing his mother in the reception room where the casket had stood, pulled at her skirts and begged, "Don't stay here! Come out, Mamma. Papa dead here all the time." Once, coming across his father's overshoes, he ran to Jessie with delighted astonishment. "Mamma!

55

Papa left his overshoes!" The fine new house on Jarvis Street was too big and too full of memories. By the end of the year Jessie, with a now drastically reduced income, moved her young family to a smaller place on nearby Ontario Street.

Ironically, the city of Toronto was *en fête* in the year of Charles Albert's death, preparing to celebrate the fifty years since its incorporation in 1834. On March sixth, the actual anniversary, the *Globe* commented: "Toronto was incorporated just fifty years ago today, and the journalist of that day thought the event just important enough to use up six lines of long primer type to acquaint the citizens with that fact." The Toronto of today would do better, said the *Globe*, but celebrations were being delayed to "the leafy month of June."

A week of festivities began on June thirtieth, with well-organized projects for each day: Military Day, Trades and Industrial Day, United Empire Loyalists' Day, the Benevolent Societies' Day, Educational Day. An arch was erected on King Street, there were parades with "gay banners and crashing music," the inevitable pyrotechnics show on the Bay, a Lieutenant-Governor's reception and a military review. Crowds thronged the streets, and the police encountered the same kind of trouble as they do today. One of them who tried to arrest a woman disturbing the peace was met by onlookers with stolid indifference to his appeals for help when she lay down, and had to wait for police reinforcements. The press summed up fifty years of progress. The *Globe* said:

The world of 1834 was in most respects very different from that of this present year of grace. Railroads were all but unknown. No steamers had crossed the Atlantic, if indeed the impossibility of such a feat had not been already *demonstrated* on scientific principles. The electric telegraph was still a thing of the future, and cheap postage was not even so much as broached.

Semi-centennial brooches in sterling and gold were offered, engraved with pictures of local architecture. The celebrations

56

ended editorially on a suitable we-must-look-ahead note of inspiration. In a book on Toronto published two years later, a writer noted similar progress. If one were to stand at the corner of King and Yonge Streets, he said:

. . . he would find carriages of every style, private and public, including phaetons, broughams, wagons, coupes, market carts, dog carts, rockaways, pony carriages and hansoms in endless variety, also drays, lorries, merchants', manufacturers', express and tradesmen's delivery wagons—all producing a scene of bustle and activity only to be witnessed in a great and prosperous city, and showing a marvellous contrast with the appearance of the streets in 1847.

Fruits of Success

The demands of the company, now Charley was gone, were far too heavy for Hart to handle alone. His second son, Chester, was appointed vice-president but Chester had little interest in the business world. His health was delicate following an early illness, and he was absorbed by religious and cultural activities, notably the Chautauqua summer programmes of education and recreation. The project had been started in the United States in 1874 by John Heyl Vincent and Lewis Miller as a Methodist Sunday school assembly and expanded in 1878 into the Chautauqua Literary and Scientific Circle.

Hart took the obvious step. He brought back from Boston his third son, Walter Edward Hart, cutting short his university career, and appointed him secretary-treasurer of the company.

Walter, who had been seven when the family moved to Cleveland, was now a tall lively bright-eyed young man of twenty. His height had prompted a jocular biographical comment: "It was at first proposed to name him Walter Massey, but this name was so evidently out of all proportion to the length of the infant that, on further consultation, the initials 'E. H.' were interpolated." Walter Edward Hart grew into a lanky boy who at fourteen was "head and shoulders above all his classmates [at Brooks' Military School in Cleveland] and was distinguished as the one who wore the longest stripes on his trousers." His interests had included chemistry ("the rate of insurance rose 50 per cent throughout the neighborhood" when he set up a laboratory at the back of the house) and photography (he owned a camera as early as 1880). Now, actively engaged in the family firm, he added verve and versatility to the energy of his father and the boldness his eldest brother had contributed.

Things were humming at the works, and Walter stepped into the breach with flair and flourish. The 1880s were years of stepped-up activity in field trials and tournaments, gala demonstrations and international exhibitions. Delivery Day, when consignments of orders arrived in towns across the country, became a banner-waving, trumpet-blowing parade of Massey implements through the streets, with civic welcome, dinners for the neighbouring farmers at which a Massey son might make a speech, and fête-day atmosphere. There were transatlantic journeys for Hart and his sons (and often Lillian) to present impressive displays of Massey machinery at the 1885 Exhibition in Antwerp, Belgium, the 1886 Indian and Colonial Exhibition in London, England, and the Paris Exposition of 1889.

Walter Massey, it seemed, had been blessed of the gods—with wealth, a happy disposition, good looks (a longer face than his brother Charles, but with the strong Massey mouth inherited from his mother, and large dark expressive eyes), a sense of humour and a kindly heart. Anything he undertook he did superbly well, and his roving interests explored every development of the age.

Behind the frantic pace of business (Hart and his sons were working ten-hour days six days a week) a warm personal life continued. For Walter's twenty-first birthday on April fourth, 1885, the family prepared a surprise party at the Toronto home they called Euclid Hall in tribute to their happy associations with the avenue they had lived on in Cleveland. "It was resolved," said *The Trip Hammer* (the company's staff magazine) facetiously, "to make one more effort to bring home to him the preposterous character of the step he was about to take. If he kept on in the course he was pursuing, nothing could save him from becoming a man." Out-of-town school friends and relatives had been arriving at the big house on the corner of Jarvis and Wellesley streets from United States cities and other parts of Canada to mark the event. "His mother, especially, as mothers will, put forth strong efforts to hold him within the enchanted circle of boyhood. She continually reminded him that it was only a few days since she held him in her arms a baby, and that it was absurd of him to act as if it were twenty-one years ago. Deaf to all entreaty, however, he kept right on."

On the eventful evening family and guests gathered in the big drawing-room with its heavy drapes, lace curtains, overstuffed furniture and red velour carpet, and turned the lights low. As Walter unsuspectingly entered the room, the lights went suddenly up. He found himself the centre of a laughing crowd, all pleading with him not to take the fatal step into manhood. "Did the vision melt his stubborn heart?" burbled *The Trip Hammer*. "No, he incontinently turned tail and ran away! Being traced to his room shortly afterwards, he was found with a man's dress coat on, and came down in a brazen and defiant manner."

The festivities continued, with music from the Massey Cornet Band and the Orchestra sounding gently from the lawn. Walter was presented with a formal address, twenty-four feet long and lavishly decorated on the underside with floral and geometric patterns. With due solemnity everyone helped him unroll the document, "read in turns by the more able-bodied members (who were carried out when exhausted)." On the following evening in the seven-hundred-seat Massey Memorial Hall at the plant, the young people presented a series of tableaux and charades, to which the employees were invited. In Hart Massey's austere religious code, the theatre was the abode of the devil: his spirited young family got around the taboo by doing their own acting, for which most of them had extraordinary talent. The lifelike manner in which Chester "bearded his cruel 'Uncle,'" (the pawnbroker) and Walter's innocent astonishment when discovered (as Guy Fawkes) beneath the Houses of Parliament brought down the house. No one managed to guess the word portrayed by the charade.

But the best gift Walter received on that momentous birthday was the presence of a special guest from Boston. Though his friends might have teasingly commented that "Mr. Massey will be remembered as the gentleman who organized a vigilance committee last summer on an Atlantic steamer for the protection of the ladies," there had been only one girl in Walter Massey's heart since he first saw Susan Denton in the fall of 1883 in Boston where he was attending the Massachusetts Institute of Technology.

Susan had been twenty-two and living with a married sister when Walter arrived as a boarder at the Boston home of her brother-in-law, Olen Carter, a professor of music at East Greenwich Academy. A tall girl with hazel eyes and honey-coloured hair that hung in natural ringlets from the bow at the nape of her neck, she had got her first glimpse of the young MIT student from Toronto through a window as he knelt on the sidewalk to fix the wheel of his penny-farthing bicycle. She "didn't much care for his looks," she told a daughter years later. Susie Denton did not lack for beaux. Sometimes they came to talk to her when she was supposed to be practising her music, and she was adept at moving her feet on the organ pedals to produce sounds that would allay suspicions of dalliance. With time she found Walter's looks improved and her interest grew. Hart and Eliza, who liked her at once, began to welcome her more and more frequently at the Massey home in Toronto.

The Massey works in the 1880s were on the outskirts of Toronto, and the workmen and their families—some fifteen hundred strong, including about fifty families who came with the firm from Newcastle—formed a small social community of their own. Though Hart, in the patriarchal manner of the times, was a stern taskmaster not noted for enlightened social attitudes, within his understanding of the relationship between employer and employee he acted strictly from what he saw as a strong sense of justice and duty. The young man who had stood firmly on his own feet in his early days, asking no favours, was now the old man who expected a workman to earn his pay. "It was a

61

Kinsale Association Library

benevolent despotism," one of his employees (whose father had worked there before him) said years later. "The old man got a reputation for meanness, but he did try to develop a family feeling in the works." He might fire on the spot a man who turned in a sloppy performance but he gave life employment to anyone injured on the job, he provided facilities for social and recreational activity, and even brought from Germany a qualified musician, Professor A. Hartmann, to lead the Massey Band. He commanded a healthy respect and, despite some justifiable bitterness, often a reluctant affection. Whispers would fly around the works when Hart Massey appeared in the shops: "The old man's in the works, did you see him? . . . He asked me about my baby . . . He sent my wife a turkey . . ."

Young Walter brought a joyous sense of fellowship to his responsibilities. Though *The Trip Hammer* was published by a volunteer committee of the employees, Walter was its business manager and associate editor under the name of "Prof. Scrub." For the thirteen issues of its existence (it merged with *Massey's Illustrated* in March, 1886) it commented brightly on national, local and domestic doings. It reported meetings of the Employees' Mutual Benefit Society formed in 1883. It urged employees to join the Workman's Library Association, for which a comfortable reading and writing room had been provided, equipped with an extensive and carefully chosen variety of current periodicals, and open at certain times to adult members of employees' families. It commended the activities of the Glee Club, the Orchestra and the Massey Band (which grew to professional status, winning prizes and regularly performing, smartly dressed in uniforms provided by the company, at skating rinks and fall fairs). It described the Sabbath School started in the Massey Memorial Hall. *The Trip Hammer* scored a scoop in its August issue by publishing the first copies of the newly completed 1885 government map of the Dominion. It also appointed as "war correspondent" one of the two employees who went off to the Riel Rebellion.

His letters brought to their readers a sometimes amusing and

62

often cliff-hanging sense of participation in events at the battle front. Describing the night of August eighteenth, 1885, correspondent Fred Harris wrote:

I was placed in picquet for the first time since leaving Qu'Appelle ... with the thermometer away down as it sometimes goes down here with the sun, there are many things about it decidedly uncomfortable . . . Fire will do to scare wolves; redskins with Winchesters are wolves of another species . . . So we do not build watchfires in the vicinity of Indians. . . . My night's watch was barren of events except once, when a bush at a short distance from my post suddenly assumed a belligerent attitude, and came near getting a bullet through it for its foolishness . . . I slept [next] night the sleep of the just. If you really want to find out what sleep is do this: Take your gun—and you had better have your great coat also—walk down Strachan Avenue, across the bridge, down the steps and out into, say the middle of the Garrison Common—time, 1 A.M. Plant yourself there and see that no Indians come ashore in their canoes from the lake, or half-breeds steal down upon you from the shadows of the Exhibition Grounds; pace slowly and noiselessly up and down through the long hours until the welcome beams of the sun and the coming of the relief guard release you from your post. Return to your camp in Trinity College grounds, breakfast, strike tent, march out to Cooksville and back again, keeping a sharp look out for Indians all the way, arriving at 5 P.M.; pitch tent—have supper—clean accoutrements—get your double blanket, also your single one, also your rubber sheet—spread them carefully on your mattress, the ground, and roll yourself up. If you had a $10,000 note coming due tomorrow, with $2.98 at your credit in your bank book, you would be asleep long before you could figure out what the manager was going to do about it. . . .

On the 23rd, as we were nearing Battleford, about 15 miles out, some of our scouts came in and reported the place full of Indians. We pushed forward as rapidly as possible and camped within three miles of the town, intending to treat the Indians to a surprise party in the early morning . . . No doubt Col. Otter had good reasons for deciding to await the morning before attacking . . . However that may be, when morning dawned there were no Indians visible, but there were innumerable evidences that they had been there. Several houses were burnt, among them the Government House, which is said to have cost $40,000. Every dwelling outside the fort was pillaged; everything of value that could be removed taken; articles too

63

bulky to be carried away were destroyed; furniture knocked to pieces; chickens, geese, pigs, etc., were killed and left lying about, destroyed apparently for destruction's sake alone. The Hudson Bay Co.'s store was burnt and its contents looted. The whole place, on the east side of the river, is a scene of utter ruin. It was exceedingly fortunate that the townspeople received warning in time to get into the fort, otherwise there might have been a bloody tale to tell. . . .

Among the many articles of household furniture smashed into kindling wood I saw a valuable piano—that is, it was a valuable one before the Indian concert was held; it might now be bought cheap. They must have had any amount of fun with that piano. They formed circles around it, danced war dances about it, all the performers who could get at the keyboard furnishing the music, then they pounded it with clubs, and as a grand finale went at it with tomahawks and so maimed and disfigured it that it is now, as one of the boys remarked, "the sickest looking piano you ever saw." I was one of a foraging party sent to the Indian reserve about fifteen miles from Battleford to bring in any portable property that might have been left behind. The village was entirely deserted; not a living thing, not even a dog to be seen. We loaded up ten wagons with stuff— flour, potatoes, etc. In the Indian huts we found all sorts of strange things. I became the happy possessor of a tom tom or Indian drum, banjo, a tanning stick, about 20 steel traps and a tomahawk; don't know whether I will be allowed to keep them or not. An Indian hut is an institution. It is built wholly of logs, mud floor, no upper storey, mud fire place in one corner. There is a kind of pit or cellar in each hut about eight foot deep and four feet square, which seems to be the receptacle for everything in the shape of refuse, and must be an extremely handy arrangement.

In one of the tepees we had a most ghastly find—the dead body of a young Indian woman, about 25 years of age, with her dead papoose by her side. The form of the mother was strapped up in blankets tied with thongs of deer skin; her face was painted in what I supposed was war paint. The papoose was laid beside her with its playthings in two baskets, one at its head and the other at its feet, for its soul, no doubt, "upon its journey to the kingdom of Ponemah." It was a most pathetic picture, and although she was only a poor Indian woman I fancy there were signs of moisture in the eyes of some of the boys as we turned away and left them lying there, the dark-skinned mother and her little child. A deep wound on her head showed that she had been murdered. We surmised that she was the wife of farm instructor Payne, and that the Indians had killed her because she refused to join them or betray her husband. After making a tour of the huts we visited Payne's house. In the barnyard among the straw we found his body where it had been left by the red fiends when they had finished their hellish work. There was a large hole in his head, and on going inside the house it was evident that he must have made a gallant resistance to his brutal foes. There was blood everywhere—blood on the floor, on the walls; books and papers smeared with the red stain; broken chairs, bedsteads, dressing-tables, all bearing the crimson splashes of murder. It was a pitiful sight to see this comfortable home so reduced in a few minutes to ruin and desolation—most pitiful to find a child's first book of lessons with her name, "Baptista Payne, Battleford, January 20th, 1884," written on the fly leaf, smeared with blood, put away perhaps after her last lesson beside her father's knee, nevermore to be opened by poor little Baptista. . . .

Payne has a fine, large house, with good furniture, and lived, I should say, in a comfortable manner. I found his diary among some other papers which I have handed over to Col. Otter. Among the many things we found none I think surprised me so much as a Toronto Mower, Harvester and Horse Rake, made by the Massey Manufacturing Company—all in good order and ready to go to work in the field.

The letter dated May third, 1885, began:

We have met the enemy, and . . . taught them a lesson they are not likely to forget . . . On Friday last, May 1st . . . Indians were reported, some 300 strong, within thirty miles of Battleford, and Col. Otter determined to see for himself what they were made of . . . The train marched or rather drove out from camp about 4 P.M. on Friday, May 1st. They held their way without incident worthy of notice, except a halt to wait for the moon to rise, until five on Saturday morning, when they came upon a lately deserted camp, with not an Indian or half-breed in sight. This was some thirty-five or forty miles from Battleford, and proved that the information received by Col. Otter was correct. The Indians had been there, and could not now be far away. A short distance farther and the scouts reported an Indian lookout, and almost immediately afterwards the tepees were sighted. B battery was at once ordered to the front, under command of Major Short, supported by 75 Mounted Police under Col. Herchmer. The trail here ascended a hill, and scarcely had the summit been reached when a volley was poured into our troops from the edge of a heavily wooded ravine some 200 yards distant. The guns were quickly unlimbered, the Police extended along the brow of the hill, and the remainder of the troops sprang to their positions at the word of command. The situation, roughly stated, seemed to be, that our troops occupied the open space across the heel of a horseshoe, while the enemy, reinforced since latest advices, and outnumbering us two to one, held points of vantage all round the shoe itself. There could scarcely be a more critical situation for raw troops to find themselves in, but they were equal to the emergency. From their front and on both flanks they were harassed by repeated volleys from the Winchesters of the Indians and half-breeds and the only wonder is that the dead and wounded were not many more. The Gatling did splendid service from the first, and must have astonished the redskins considerably by the rapidity and deadliness of its fire.

They did not remain long enough exposed, however, to obtain a full insight into its working, but sought cover in the adjoining woods, where they were treated to a dose or two of shell by way of a change. The fighting now became general all along our front. The first man to fall was Corporal Sleigh, of the Mounted Police, and the ambulance corps of the Queen's Own soon found that they were not to remain idle spectators of the fray. After about half an hour's fighting the enemy was reinforced in front, and with extraordinary rashness actually made a dash at the Gatling gun. Major Short, however, did not propose to stand that sort of thing, and, charging down upon the rebels, drove them before him easily. The Gatling was now turned on the Indian camp, some 600 yards distant, and created a commotion in that establishment unexampled in its history. And so the fight went on hour after hour, our brave three hundred holding their own, and more than holding it against the horde of savages and half-breeds, 700 of them who encircled them on every hand. But the circle must be broken, and to that prince of scouts, Charlie Ross, was entrusted the task of breaking it. It was a duty after his own heart, and most nobly he performed it. Calling for volunteers, among whom were twelve of the Queen's Own, he led them up the hill against the enemy's position to the right, clearing them out in short order, and driving them from their vantage ground back to their own lines in front of our position. This was accomplished without the loss of a single man, and the noble fellows were cheered on all sides as the enemy flew before them. In this charge the horse of Little Poplar was captured. This movement not only relieved our right which had been greatly annoyed by the fire from the hill but compelled the enemy to show themselves in the open, and besides those who fell before our rifles in the charge, their flying ranks were decimated by the Gatling as they exposed themselves in their hasty retreat. Attention was now turned toward the left, where a company of half-breeds had posted themselves in a deep ravine, and sixty men of the Battleford Rifles and Queen's Own went at it with so good a will that in an hour, they had cleared the ravine and followed the enemy until they found themselves in danger from our own shells, when they took to cover, and, like the Irishman at Donnybrook, "wherever they saw a head" they "hit it" if they could. About noon the rebels made a rally in front, but were unable to face the fire that was poured into them, and soon retired to their familiar cover. Col. Otter now having accomplished all he could hope to under the circumstances resolved to retire, the Queen's Own being detailed to cover the retreat. . . .

So the battle ended, the result being, I should think, a serious blow to Poundmaker and his allies, making it clear to them that even with the advantage of numbers and position they were no match for Canadian troops. Their dead must be nearly 100, but the number is at present unknown. . . .

I had a lot of "relics" but the boys have "hooked" them nearly all. I have presented Capt. Delamere with my big war drum, the regimental kit not being capacious enough to contain it. We have not heard anything from General Middleton. It is reported that he has met Riel and whipped him, but we know nothing definite. . . .

"I have met Captain Dickens here, son of the great novelist," wrote Fred, never one to miss a newsworthy item, "and have had several long chats with him. He is, I think, strikingly like his father, judging from portraits I have seen of that prince of humorists, and has proven himself a good soldier and a brave man."

His next letter was dated June 2:

On May 25th, shortly after breakfast a scout rode into camp and reported that a string of waggons containing half-breeds was on its way in our direction. Soon in the distance they could be seen winding down the hill towards the bridge that spans the Battle River below the town. A white flag borne at the front of the procession indicated a peaceful intent, and their arrival was awaited with considerable interest.

Kinsale Association
        Library

At first it was thought, as it approached nearer, that they were accompanied by a horse fiddle band executing selections of the most heartrending description, expressive of the feelings of the conquered as they came to bow themselves before the great white chief who had overcome them . . . I had never yet heard anything so inexpressibly dismal as the sounds, which louder and louder, now came on towards us through the pure morning air. What do you suppose the music was? Only the Red River carts, which never go any place without an accompaniment of this character. I had heard one or two before but here were over fifty all squeaking and wailing and groaning in concert, and I assure you the effect was immense. But the carts were only a small part of the menagerie; there were the ponies and the oxen, and the harness and the camp equipage—the tepees, the stoves, the stovepipes, the beds, the furniture, the old men, the old women, the mothers, the papooses, the middle aged men, the young men, the maidens, the children. . . . They were not long in making themselves, to all appearance, quite at home, and some of the boys paid them a visit shortly afterward and had a talk with some of their more prominent men. They all persevere in asserting that Poundmaker kept them prisoners, and that they did not want to fight the whites. . . .

Things were settling down into their accustomed monotony, when suddenly, like lightning from a clear sky (if you're not particular about your similes), there dashed into the town a painted savage on an Indian pony and announced to the general, who rode out to meet him, that the big Indian himself, Poundmaker, and his braves were also coming in to lay down their arms. This was exciting news and everybody was at once on the qui vive. Some of the men were ordered under arms lest treachery should be intended, and every eye was turned towards the point of the compass where the Indians were expected to make their appearance. We had not long to wait. The dusky procession soon came in sight, on the trail close by what was once Government House. . . .

Some of the horses were without collars, the waggon poles being fastened in some mysterious fashion to straps about their necks, and pointing upwards over their ears—traces of deer hide were tied to these straps and fastened to the whipple-trees in the rear; no reins, drivers running alongside, yelling and pounding the poor animals until the air seemed filled with brandished goads and Indian yells. The procession came in this manner into camp and halted amid acclamations. Poundmaker and his chiefs having stated the object of their visit, their arms and

68

horses were taken from them and preparations were made for a big talk. . . .

They all tried to show that their intentions were at all times of the most innocent character, and that when they murdered men, burnt houses and pillaged the country they were compelled to do so by Riel or somebody else, who of course ought to be punished. General Middleton gave it as his deliberate opinion that they were humbugs; that their explanations were lies, and ended by ordering Poundmaker, Yellow-Mud-Blanket, Breaking-through-the-Ice and Lean-Man into custody, and telling the others they had better go back to their reserves, behave themselves and try to cultivate the land. . . .

Poundmaker himself maintained the reputation of his race in this respect, no outward sign being visible of the thoughts within; not a muscle quivered, and he might have been a figure of stone, so stolidly did he listen to the indignant words of the pale-face chief . . . He is really a splendid looking fellow, an ideal red man of the forest . . . It would be almost a pity to hang such a man, and yet it would never do to allow traitors and rebels to escape punishment because of their good looks . . .

It is said that troubles never come singly. I believe it. We had scarcely purged the camp of the presence of Poundmaker's following when a third procession, more ridiculous if possible than either of the others, was heard afar off among the hills and slopes of the Saskatchewan. I say heard, because you can always hear a procession of Red River carts long before you can see it. Again arose the inexpressibly dismal wailings with which we were now familiar, and it was thought at first that our late guests were returning. But it turned out to be another band led by Moosomin, a notable Indian chief, who had hitherto held aloof from the rebels, and who wished to give the General personal assurances of the continued loyalty of himself and people. Well they came in bearing a white flag with "Moosomin Indians" painted on it, led by the chief himself in a buckboard drawn by a team of Indian ponies. The harness was manufactured of "shagnappie," and was most fearfully and wonderfully put together. Besides the harness the ponies were caparisoned in three strings of loud, old-fashioned sleigh bells, which imparted a lofty dignity to the equipage of the chieftain and served as a distinguishing mark of his position. The fearful clatter of these bells was a fitting prelude to the Babel following close behind, to be heard easily a mile away. The mariner of ancient mythology who filled the ears of his sailors with cotton and so saved them from the lure of the syren [sic] was a man with a level head; but his artifice would have availed nothing in our case. Whole bales of cotton would have been insufficient to shut out the awful sounds which now burst upon us in all their intensity. You have heard the old fable of the "waggon cursing its driver" . . . The volume of imprecations indulged in by a string of Red River carts devoid of lubricant, is a sad commentary on the missionary enterprise of the nineteenth century. And if to this you add the bawling of oxen and the yells of their Indian drivers as they ran beside the poor animals pounding them with ox-goads, you may, if you have a vivid imagination, conceive some faint idea of the reality. On they came, Moosomin leading. On shrieked the carts, some laden with women and children, others with necessaries. Some of the old squaws were so shrivelled and dried up and wrinkled that one could scarcely believe them at first to be human beings. Then the papooses clad for the most part in dirt, and having the most comical appearance. Then the younger men and warriors mounted on horses and wearing blankets and moccasins and nothing else, if I except a stovepipe hat once in a while, stuck round with feathers, and evidently feeling its degradation.

On their arrival home at the end of the war the two warriors, Privates Harris and Booth, were given a public reception in the Massey Memorial Hall at the works, with a musical entertainment, a question period during which the audience showered the boys with all kinds of queries about their experiences, and an adulatory address read by the chairman, who concluded:

In all her history the city has never seen so grand a sight as on the day when her "boys" came home. You, gentlemen, have seen it—it was prepared for you. You felt your hearts throb with honest pride and exultation as you marched through the miles of welcome which greeted you, from voice, from triumphal arch, from flying banner and decorated street. From the shouts of admiring fellow citizens; from the sweet five hundred child-voices blending together in a harmonious welcome home. What need, therefore, that we should add more? Toronto is proud of her soldiers.

Meanwhile there were field trials and fall fairs to prepare for, and not only in Canada. In 1860 Hart had won a silver medal at the Prince of Wales Exhibition in Montreal, the highest prize for a threshing machine. The 1862 catalogue had listed prizes won all over the world including gold medals of honour, from such places as Paris, Greifswald in Mecklenburg, and Cincinnati, Ohio. At the Vienna Exhibition in 1873 Hart had earned the decoration of The Imperial Order of Francis Joseph for his mowers and reapers. In 1876, at the Philadelphia Exhibition held to celebrate the centennial of the Declaration of Independence, the hundreds and thousands of visitors who gaped at the strange contrivance called the telephone, invented by the Canadian Alexander Graham Bell, could also see agricultural machinery that had won highest honours for another Canadian, Hart Massey.

In 1883 the Toronto Light Binder had been demonstrated for the Governor General of Canada, the Marquis of Lorne, and his lady, Princess Louise, the Queen's fourth daughter, at a spectacular garden party held next door to the works in the Toronto Asylum ground, where the Massey Cornet Band provided music. In 1886, on the same site, a display showing the four ages of reaping was put on for the public "in a field of badly-tangled oats." An old Staffordshire man wielded the sickle of the first period. "A city gentleman who once earned his bread by its use" demonstrated the old-fashioned cradle. For the third period, a Wood's reaper "made by H. A. Massey, Esq., at Newcastle in 1865, and which has cut for 22 seasons," showed it was still in excellent working condition.

But THE TRIUMPH OF THE AGE was the Toronto Light Binder Number 3. To show how easily the machine worked, a number of amateurs lined up to run it: "reporters, doctors, lawyers, and ladies alternately," among them Charley's widow Jessie and Chester's young bride of six months. (Chester's interest in Chautauqua had included Anna Vincent, the small dark-eyed high-spirited half-sister of its co-founder, John Heyl Vincent.) The Toronto *Mail* marvelled at machines that could be run by a lady with "not so much as a speck of dust upon her elegant toilet," and suggested that "this somewhat took the conceit out of the gentlemen who had been pluming themselves upon their agricultural skill. It was, indeed, truly marvellous to see a great swath of grain cut, bound into sheaves, and the sheaves deposited over the field in heaps by the agency of a delicate lady."

Since Charles Albert's tragic death in February, 1884, Jessie Massey had been living quietly in the narrow brick semi-detached house at 288 Ontario Street. Now, after three years of widowhood, she was ready for marriage again: she had fallen in love with a young bank clerk, John Haydn Horsey. They were married on June second, 1887, and Hart, who loved his son Charley's children and had sat beside the youngest one, Bessie (not quite six), for the wedding breakfast, came up with a wonderful idea. To allow Jessie and her new husband a period of freedom, and since the three older children were in boarding-school, why should not Bessie and her brother Bertie, now nearly seven, come to stay with their grandparents for a while?

Bessie was enchanted with life at the Jarvis Street mansion. After you went beneath the portico with its raised flat slab of stone for mounting into carriages, you passed over a tesselated marble floor to the big front hall from which the stairs ran up to the next landing. In the centre of the hall a tiny fountain poured sparkles of water into a pool, and small faces could press against the glass walls of the raised octagonal container to gaze at an enchanted world where goldfish swam through drowned castles. There was the great clock on the landing, which grandfather wound every night at nine o'clock by pulling down the weights, but it was not often you saw this when you were only six and eight o'clock was your bedtime. There was Dick, the fascinating coloured coach-man who would let you watch in the stable while he rubbed the horses till their coats shone, or washed the carriage down. There was the importance of driving to church on Sundays behind the big horses, sitting demure and ladylike between grandfather and grandmother, in high-button boots, cloak and bonnet, and nice little kid gloves.

Sometimes grandfather would take Bessie to the works, where

she would spend the whole day, going downstairs at noon for a hot dinner with the janitor's wife. She even had a job of her own —swatting flies with a folded newspaper. Every evening there was the exciting ritual of meeting grandfather at the door. After he had washed, he would play tag around the garden or pretend to be a bear in the parlour, crawling on the red velour carpet and letting her ride on his back. In summer they would often take tea on the lawn under a huge Japanese umbrella. In winter they would stand in the wide front window and watch the young gentlemen of Toronto and their ladies race their red cutters down the icy road on Sunday afternoon, while grandfather muttered at the desecration of the Sabbath. In the house built to the north of grandfather's, Bessie would visit Uncle Chester and Aunt Anna, often allowed the important privilege of minding a new young cousin born on February twentieth, 1887, and named Charles Vincent (he would drop the Charles when he was older). And, of course, there were the two dashing uncles, effervescent Walter and tall athletic twenty-year-old Fred, who was a student at the University of Toronto and who threw himself with gusto into endlessly interesting occupations. He liked experimenting with strange plants in the conservatory. He careered along garden paths on his bicycle, and produced odd mechanical gadgets at his workbench. He built fancy houses for the various pets he kept, whistling off-key all the time as he worked.

Fred had never been interested in music, but his music-loving family teased until he agreed to study the flute. Never one to do things by halves, he engaged an instructor and practised assiduously (and, one is tempted to think, relentlessly) at every opportunity during the day, including before breakfast and just before retiring. After a couple of terms he was expert enough to join a small orchestra, and found he had learned to enjoy music in all its forms.

Toward the middle of 1887 it had been apparent that Walter Massey's hectic activities—work at the plant and his heavy involvement in employee welfare—were affecting his health.

Charley's untimely death stood as a warning. Hart decided that Walter should take a long trip abroad and—with his usual shrewd thinking—that he could combine business with his pleasure and attend to the opening of an Australian market for Massey machines. Six binders ordered by a Melbourne dealer at the 1886 Indian and Colonial Exhibition in London were sent ahead in the care of a company agent, and on August seventeenth, 1887, the Massey party left Toronto on the first leg of what was to be a ten-month world tour. In the party with Walter were Fred, breaking his university course to act as his brother's aide; fair-haired, gentle Lillian (still unmarried at thirty-three, her possible beaux frightened off by Hart's fierce paternalism)—and Susan Denton from Boston. The two ladies accompanied "the boys" only as far as San Francisco. There had been some hope in Walter's heart that he might marry his Susan and make this a honeymoon trip; but Hart had thought otherwise. With the usual family deference to the old man, the marriage was postponed. "The only one who ever stood up to grandfather," his granddaughter Bessie remembered, "was Chester's wife, Anna Vincent. Very quietly and gently she showed him she intended to run her own life. He had a very great respect for her."

Travel and Tragedy

"The boys" were adventurous travellers and both kept copious notes of their experiences. A spate of cables announced their safe arrival in Honolulu, Auckland, Sydney and other Australian ports, Port Said, the Holy Land, Naples and finally Britain. Letters followed, most of them published in *Massey's Illustrated* minutely and vividly recording the scenes, impressions, history and economics of the places visited. Dozens of photographs illustrated the trip. "W. E. H. Massey, one of the sons of the president of the Massey Manufacturing Company," said the Toronto *Evening Telegram* on May twelfth, 1888, "is now on his way around the world taking views." Walter's buoyant curiosity about everything enriched the trip immensely. His searching eyes missed little of interest. "I did not look for such a pretty city as it is," he wrote of Winnipeg. Victoria and Seattle bothered him. The first he found to be "like most Pacific Coast Towns, a decidedly 'wicked' city, and there is a great need of moral reform." In the other, "intemperance prevailed to a shocking extent."

At Portland the party divided, Walter going by train and stage on the quicker but more uncomfortable overland route in order to meet a Massey agent, the others going down the coast by steamer. He drank in the spectacular scenery and the experience of a new and strange environment—a sunset on snow-covered Mount Rainier, "the large and elegant ferries" in San Francisco, and "the clang of numerous street car and cable car bells." He found Santa Barbara overcrowded and dusty but Los Angeles was a very pretty place, with "a great many beautiful avenues,

75

fine residences and elegant private grounds, adorned with palms, semi-tropical trees, shrubs and flowers of great variety. There are many orange groves in the vicinity, too."

Monterey, and especially Pacific Grove, two and a half miles distant, pleased the travellers even more.

The town of Monterey itself is small and very antiquated, most of the old buildings and houses being of Spanish adobe style— with queer old tiled roofs—and rapidly coming to ruin. One which was torn down just before my arrival, supposed to be nearly a hundred years old, hadn't a single nail in its framework, the corners being fastened with wooden pins and the rafters bound on with raw hide. The great Del Monte Hotel, which was burned last spring, was located half a mile from the town, and has since been rebuilt on an even more magnificent scale, something like six hundred guest bedrooms.

Pacific Grove was "an especially desirable spot for health seekers. No spirituous liquors can be sold or given away, all amusements of a doubtful character are prohibited, and all must be quiet after ten thirty P.M." Here the small party swam and collected shells along the splendid rocky coast and went for drives, passing the "Seal Rocks,"

which are literally covered with these curious, howling or barking and bad-smelling animals of the sea. They are plainly visible from shore, climbing up and down the rocks, basking in the sun or sporting in the water. The bones of whales are washed ashore on the Monterey coast in large quantities—some vertebrae and ribs being of enormous size. I saw several rustic arches at the gates of cottages made by planting and entwining together two of these immense ribs. The effect was decidedly more curious than artistic.

Though the travellers had left Toronto in mid-August, they did not embark (on the S.S. *Australia* from San Francisco) until November eighth. They had made leisurely progress by train to Vancouver and down the west coast, delayed several times by the illness either of Walter or of Lillian, who was not strong. At Glacier, in the Rockies, where they had to stay for several days,

Walter and Susan enjoyed the chance to wander off together on delightful walks through the heavy forest to the foot of the shining glacier. "The green tints of the ice are extremely pretty, but in the glaring sunlight it is almost too brilliant to look upon," wrote Walter. The short stopover in Santa Barbara, California, was caused by an attack of malaria Walter suffered, and there were the few days of relaxation in Santa Monica and Monterey before the reluctant parting. "It adds none to the mirthfulness of the occasion," Walter wrote mournfully, "to have friends amongst the crowd on the wharf, whom you don't expect to see again for months, waving their fond adieux." Particularly if one of the friends was Susan.

The beauty of their final departure from "San Francisco's great harbor, with its islands and surrounding rocky heights" was not entirely lost on Walter but other considerations became suddenly intrusive:

We had not more than fairly passed out of the celebrated Golden Gate when great rolling Pacific swells of unusual size began to seriously disturb the equilibrium of our ship, which seemed to have a wonderful capacity for rolling. There was more than enough to occupy my attention below—the best part of the first three days being devoted to the study of stomach economy.

In Honolulu the travellers met King Kalakaua I.

He is very well educated, speaks English fluently, and is regarded as quite an orator in his own language. He has made the tour of the world and has considerable administrative ability. Like most of his countrymen he is fond of amusement and inclined to take an easy life. Like the Prince of Wales, he is the patron of boating, yachting and jockey clubs and agricultural societies. Queen Kapiolaui is spoken of by all as a lady of great amiability, and she has done much to comfort her afflicted subjects in the leprosy hospital. Ioalani Palace, the royal residence, is a large, handsome structure in the heart of the city, and bears a striking contrast to the grass huts of their great predecessor Kamehameha 1st. The palace is guarded by a very miniature army, neatly uniformed and equipped.

Walter was also much interested in the Royal Hawaiian Band, "a particularly fine musical organization of 35 to 40 pieces," and the Hawaiians' love of flowers.

Auckland, in New Zealand, he wrote, "was 'a rest' indeed after the lawless and immoral Sabbaths of the Pacific Coast. There were no Sunday papers, no street cars, saloons were closed (*back* doors and front) and a general peacefulness and quiet prevailed." A visit to the hot springs at Rotorua and the Maori village of Whakarewarewa amazed and delighted them.

Their time in Australia was so crowded with business and sightseeing, with a short rest in the quiet little Blue Mountains resort of Mount Victoria in New South Wales, that the next letter was not written until three months later, from mid-Indian Ocean, on board the S.S. *Lusitania*. The brothers had crossed Tasmania from Hobart to Launceston by a train they found amusing. "The gauge is only 3'6" and hence the cars are very small and narrow—certainly no wider than a Toronto Yonge Street car but somewhat longer." Melbourne surprised them:

I was quite prepared to find Melbourne a big city, but not the grand metropolis that it is, with fine wide streets lined with magnificent buildings of the most solid character—streets that are admirably paved and kept scrupulously clean, and which would put to shame our Toronto thoroughfares. As one walks about the city everywhere he will see the greatest life of activity, reminding him of the bustle and busy aspects of a large American city. Cable cars have entirely supplanted the use of the ordinary street cars, and Melbourne has the most nearly perfect and the most extensive cable car system in existence.

The new branch office of the company that the brothers established in Melbourne, Walter noted, was the most distant office from Massey headquarters nearly eleven thousand miles away.

Sydney, older, more crowded and dingier than Melbourne, was, for all this, "a great, wealthy and wonderful city," its greatest boast (of course!) "its most splendid harbor, which is claimed to have no equal for general excellence and beauty"

78

and "the beautiful park and botanical gardens, both of which command charming views of the spacious harbor, dotted here and there with pretty little islands."

Egypt, Palestine, England and home lay ahead of "the boys," and Walter busily recorded everything within range of his eager eyes: the gulls, the flying fish, the phosphorescent light on the water, "the sight of the rugged top of the sacred Mount Sinai in the Gulf of Suez," the church service held on deck.

At the ringing of the fore and aft bells—the church bells at sea—those who desired assembled on the quarterdeck from all parts of the ship for divine service; and on this occasion the second class and steerage passengers, who at other times are separated by strong barriers, came to the first cabin deck, and there in one assemblage—a beautiful thought—the rich and the poor united in the worship of God, who is no respecter of persons.

The Holy Land, as might have been expected, roused a passionate emotion in the hearts of the deeply religious young travellers. They dropped biblical names with reverential awe: Bethlehem, Jerusalem, the Tomb of Rachel, the Mount of Olives, the Church of the Holy Sepulchre and the Chapel of the Nativity. Walter was moved to see shepherds leading their sheep in the same way as in biblical times, and to Susan in Boston he sent a small bouquet of pressed field flowers—"some flowers from the hills of Judea"—picked on April second, 1888. A daughter treasures them still.

In Jaffa they had an unfortunate experience.

We had scarcely set foot on land when an insolent Turkish official stepped up and demanded a passport in a haughty manner. Passport we had none, being told it was unnecessary, though we had its equivalent, and more shouldn't have been required, as we were afterwards informed. But no, he must have a Turkish passport. I tried to explain matters through my dragoman (interpreter and guide, whom I had brought from Egypt) and get him to allow us to go to the hotel and get breakfast, till he could see the British Consul—a claim I had a perfect right to make, since he couldn't leave his post to go to the Consul at once. However, he would scarcely listen to me and threatened to send me back to the boat. To be so insolently treated by a petty clerk put my control over my temper to its fullest test. Finally he consented to allow our dragoman to go to the British Consul while we were kept in the guard house for over an hour, and an armed Turkish soldier sitting by our side! The first time we had ever been incarcerated! In due time our dragoman returned with the British Consul, who came to the rescue with his whole retinue of servants. The manner in which the Consul opened up his batteries of Arabic upon the Turkish official was very pleasing to my ears. We were released very shortly.

The unpleasant incident was over, but it had a sequel. The Egyptian dragoman was destined to enter the lives of the Masseys again at a later date.

In London, after a storm along the coast of Crete that inevitably recalled St. Paul's experience in the same waters, older brother Chester met them, and there were business details to attend to. In May, 1887, an office had been opened in London with Hart's second cousin Frederick Isaiah Massey (a Civil War veteran and formerly treasurer of the Dubuque Iron Works) as European branch manager. Chester was faithfully fulfilling his responsibilities in a business for which he had little inclination. His interests lay much more strongly in cultural and religious fields. He had no illusions about the importance of his conscientious attention to a business with which he had only a superficial concern. "I made a momentous decision today," he once told a friend with gentle irony. "I ordered all the inkwells closed." An associate of later years wrote of the early days of the London branch office, "I can see him now, tall, thin and pale, at one end of a table and myself at the other, wheeling it from office to office along the corridors of the Queen Victoria Street office."

A quick trip from London to Sheffield aroused in Walter the reflection:

How paradoxical [that] much of the steel used in the works is purchased from Sheffield, taken out to Canada, manufactured into harvesting machinery, and sent back there to be sold. The fact that Toronto harvesting machinery is sold throughout

80

Europe almost under the eyes of English and German manufactories in the same line, is plain evidence to me that well-paid and skilled Canadian labor can more than compete with the "cheap labor" of England and the "pauper labor" as it is frequently styled, of the Continent.

Then, after visiting Edinburgh, where the Forth Bridge was in course of construction, and a brief glimpse of "the lovely green shores of the Emerald Isle" at Londonderry, the travellers put out into bad weather on the final lap of the journey. On June fourteenth, 1888, with the coast of Newfoundland in sight, Walter wrote nostalgically, "We shall have travelled between thirty-five and forty thousand miles when we arrive home, and have gone around the world . . . I shall be rejoiced again to set foot on Canadian soil."

Walter and Fred arrived in Toronto at the end of June with fanfare and jubilation, met at the station by a host of relatives and friends and the Massey Band. Even in small Bessie's mind the occasion remained memorable, with laughter and chatter and all lights on in the big house. But for Walter, homecoming meant just one thing. When he saw Susan again, he clasped around her wrist a gold bracelet from Hawaii (she would never take it off again) inscribed with the words *Me Ke Aloe Nui Pau Ole* ("I pledge thee everlasting love"). They were tired of waiting. Two weeks later, on July eleventh, 1888, they were married in Lowell, Massachusetts, in the home of a Denton sister whose husband, the Reverend Willard Perrin (a Harvard scholar and athlete who was to be a tower of strength in later years), performed the ceremony before a flower-decked altar in the parlour, itself gay with flowers and a floral heart bearing the initials *M* and *D*.

Susan was beautiful in a dress of heavy cream corded silk extending to a train, with boned bodice and fine lace at the neck falling over rows of pearls. The pointed waistline was outlined in silk cord, and pearls bordered the elbow-length sleeves. A hooped underskirt built out the back of the dress, and the front of the full skirt was slit to show a panel of lace. Walter's wedding gift was a diamond pin, and around the bride's neck was a necklace from Egypt. She wore a full-length tulle veil and carried in kid-gloved hands a bouquet of roses and maidenhair fern. Walter's wedding attire included smart suspenders of cream silk embroidered with flowers and leaves in tones of brown and gold.

Lillian was bridesmaid, Fred was best man, three young Carter nieces were maid-of-honour and train-bearers, and the wedding march was especially composed by Susan's brother-in-law, Olen Carter. When the wedded couple left for the Parker House in Boston where they would spend the night before the honeymoon in the White Mountains, Montreal and the Thousand Islands, Susan found she had forgotten something. The coachman, who was superstitious, refused to drive them back except by a different route to avoid bad luck.

Back in Toronto, Fred Victor returned to the university for his second year, the bridal couple moved into a suite in the Jarvis Street house, and Walter took up once again his heavy responsibilities with the Massey Manufacturing Company. While his administrative abilities were outstanding, it was in the advertising and publications of the firm that Walter found the happiest expression of his personality. He was having fun with *Massey's Illustrated*. By 1885 the company had its own printing department with two presses, one an eight-roller cylinder press that could print eight pages of the magazine at a time and turn out more than one thousand complete copies an hour. Walter packed *Massey's Illustrated* with cartoons, comment and information. Keeping its readers up to date with sprightly well-illustrated copy on every Massey development, every Massey success, the magazine's pages came alive as well with Walter's own exuberant curiosity about anything and everything.

In 1886 *Massey's Illustrated* went into a new dress—new size, better paper, better type and superior engravings. Through handbills and advertisements in local papers, Walter campaigned vigorously for subscribers:

Do you like good pictures? Are you fond of good crisp reading? Would a finely illustrated paper filled with items of interest to the family be a welcome monthly visitor to your home? If so, send in your name on a post card and receive a specimen copy of the NEW MASSEY'S ILLUSTRATED, post free, and see what you think of it. There will be Notes on Travel. A Beautifully Illustrated Story each month. Editorial Comments. General Items on Things of Interest to the Farmer. A Department for the Household, conducted by a lady of prominence. Something for Young People. Review of Chief Events of the Month in a Nutshell. Latest Harvesting Machinery News. The Poultry Yard, Live Stock, etc. Wit, Humour and Wisdom, etc., etc.

The magazine usually had a green cover but sometimes came out in four colours (with an illustrated article telling how this was done). There is reason to believe that "Aunt Tutu," who conducted the "Department for the Household," and offered how-to-do-it instructions for A Neat Work Bag, A Sweeping-Cap, A Hair-Pin Receiver, was Susan Massey herself. Walter's enterprise in presenting a "Universal Crop Report" gathered by telegraph and questionnaire from all over the world in July, 1890, earned him praise from the big Toronto dailies. Lively stories and poems were a forerunner of a more ambitious literary experiment, *Massey's Magazine*, which in 1896 began publishing contributions from Canadians who later became eminent in arts and letters.

There was a "Clubbing List" by which subscribers could get *Massey's Illustrated* and one or more other publications at a reduced price, and premiums to attract more sales: "Girls, you can earn some very beautiful holiday presents by getting a few more subscribers to the ILLUSTRATED. It will be easy work. Try it. Look over the handsome Premium List carefully."

In "Editorial Comment," Walter cheerfully expounded his

progressive views on all manner of subjects. He even ran comic strips.

Though life for the two little Massey grandchildren, Bertie and Bessie, was exciting, a certain lack began to develop. The two fabulous uncles had filled the house with fascinating objects from far-off lands—assegais and ostrich eggs, tiny models of biblical buildings, fragments of ancient tapestries, third- and fourth-century Coptic tunics, alabaster perfume bottles from Rome, a gladiator's helmet, even Egyptian mummies, which made Bessie shiver. Even live monkeys. Half a dozen of these lived behind a wall of wire mesh in a whitewashed shed at the end of the garden. Moses (whose "wife" was named Zipporah) was allowed out on a leash until the day when Bessie offered him a peanut and he grabbed at her little white apron. Grandmother Massey, understandably scared, vetoed any further freedom for Moses.

The house was full of laughter, the uncles joked and frolicked with the children and played tag in the garden. Gentle, blue-eyed Aunt Lilly told them stories and let them look at the doll she had had when she was as small as Bessie, and there was the lovely new Aunt Susan who sorted their underwear (four sets for each season) and helped look after them. "She was the most beautiful girl I ever saw," Bessie recalled. "No photograph ever did her justice."

But the little boy and girl were pining for their mother.

Jessie and Haydn Horsey had moved to a house on Bloor Street near Bedford Road (it was then on the outskirts of Toronto) and wanted the children with them. Hart, who dearly loved these children of his lost son, was reluctant to let them go. No matter how Jessie tried, she could get no satisfaction from him. On a couple of occasions the children were driven to visit her by Dr. N. A. Powell, Elvira Massey's son. Once when Jessie visited 515 Jarvis Street near Bessie's bedtime, the little girl threw such a tantrum when the nurse came to remove her at eight o'clock, biting and scratching and kicking, that the woman left the next day.

Jessie, at last, had had enough of waiting. On a day in June, dressed in her wine-coloured velvet with the lace fichu down the front, she hired a cab, drove to the school where the children were in class, and asked the principal if she might see them. When they came down the broad stairs, she took them by the hand and led them out to the cab. In the small enclosed space, with the curtains drawn and an atmosphere of conspiracy, she asked them solemnly would they like to come back and live with her again.

Neither of them hesitated. "Yes, yes," they cried. "We want to live with you, Mamma."

"Think well," Jessie said anxiously, while the horse shuffled, rattling its harness, and the leather upholstery creaked. "You won't have as much as grandfather can give you. You will have to do without many things."

"I don't care," said eight-year-old Bessie defiantly. "I'd rather be with you."

Jessie hugged her two young children to her, eyes filled with sudden tears, and ordered the coachman to drive back to Bloor Street. Then she sent him to the Jarvis Street house with a note to say that the children were in good hands. She kept her children, but with nothing more than the clothes on their back: deeply offended, Hart refused to send a single one of their possessions. For long evenings afterwards, while the children were closely watched and never allowed out unattended for fear their grandfather would reclaim them, Jessie made them complete new wardrobes, sewing by hand with tiny loving stitches.

Though tariff protection had helped the implement manufacturers of Canada during "the long depression" that had begun around 1873, the Massey firm had, with other industrial concerns, been forced to cut expenses to the bone in order to keep going. In a city full of people suffering from the effects

Kinsale Association
Library

of unemployment, the struggle of seemingly wealthy companies to stay afloat were unappreciated. Hart Massey, whose own fortune had been largely built by personal hard work and integrity, became an unpopular symbol of the uncaring rich. Thrift was interpreted as meanness, hard-headed business practice as grinding down the poor. "Like many other superior people," said a newspaperman who knew the Toronto of those days, "the Masseys were subject to the hostility from people who were inferior, so that everything good they tried to do was derided as hypocrisy. 'Those Masseys flaunting their wealth again' was the reception given to the really generous gifts they made to the city." Clinging desperately to one of the few industries that had kept its head above water, the employees railed at the low wages and shut-downs. The farmers, equally distressed, complained about the prices of necessary agricultural machinery, mortgaged their farms to buy the implements, and blamed the manufacturers. "From Masseyism," a disgruntled letter-to-the-editor said, "good Lord defend us!"—though some letters from farmers were published expressing gratitude for Massey terms of payment.

Even skilled workmen could get little more than a dollar a day, and the heating plant engineers at twelve dollars a week were considered to be plutocrats. Hart's ruthlessness after a strike —he regarded it as a failure of the men to accept their part of the responsibilities of the employer-employee relationship and refused to re-employ many of them—poisoned the atmosphere. Some papers were antagonistic but the Toronto *Telegram* of September twenty-second, 1894, in a call to "Be Fair," wrote:

All the editorial yowling at the Masseys and through them at the whole agricultural implement industry is extremely tiresome. An enlightened self-interest first brought the Masseys to this city. They have prospered here, and the city has profited by their prosperity. If the city owes them nothing, they owe the city nothing. The Masseys have treated Toronto quite as well as Toronto has treated them.

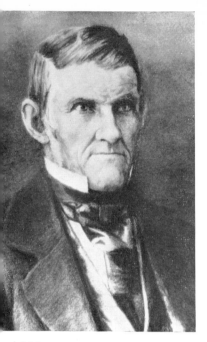

...niel Massey

Mrs. Daniel Massey

Charles Albert, Jessie, Chester, Eliza Ann, Fred Victor, Hart, Lillian & William Massey

Jessie Arnold Massey

Charles Albert Massey

Susan Denton
(Mrs. Walter Massey), 1868

Walter Massey, 1873

Manitoba Colonist Supplement.

THE MASSEY MANUFACTURING CO., TORONTO, ONT., CANADA.

The Old Newcastle Works, 1864.

(Printed from an old Stereotype used in the Catalogue of that year.)

These shops, as they appear above, together with a large stock of finished machines, were totally destroyed by
fire and immediately rebuilt in 1864.

**New Malleable Iron Foundry, with Pattern and Experimental
Departments annexed.**

This is the best equipped Malleable Shop in the Dominion.

Anna Vincent Massey, Walter Massey, Chester Massey and Susan Massey

Bishop Vincent, Lillian, Vincent, Chester and Anna Vincent Massey

Hart Massey was little troubled by the embittered criticism. The course he pursued was, in his code, just and proper, a code under which those who earned them were entitled to keep their rewards. Meanwhile, gold medals for performance continued to be collected all over the world by Massey machines. In 1889 the Paris Universal Exhibition was to give him one of his greatest triumphs.

He had been to Paris before, when his machinery had been officially chosen to represent Canadian manufacturing at the 1867 Exhibition in that city. Here the country boy from the log cabin of backwoods Canada had been introduced to the cosmopolitan life of the Old World. One wonders what his Methodist outlook made of the easy gaiety and "sinful" pleasures he could not have failed to see around him. Hart was not so much of an evangelist as—like his ancestor John—"an upright man." One senses that he would waste little more than a frowning shake of the head for those foolish enough to risk their immortal souls on such trivialities, and concentrate on the common-sense realities of life as he had charted it for himself.

The 1867 Paris Exhibition had been a glittering affair of novelty and excitement. The Champs de Mars was given over to its buildings, and its main building, the "palace," was made up of eight elliptical galleries intersected by sixteen avenues radiating from a central garden, each about five hundred feet long and named—as in Rue de Canada—for participating countries. The way of life of various nations was depicted in separate buildings. The Russian stables and post-house had stalls for twenty horses, put through their paces daily by a groom in the livery of the Czar. Visitors stood spellbound before models of the Roman catacombs and a Turkish mosque. All around the walls of the palace's seven concentric ovals clustered restaurants offering food from every country, prepared and served by nationals in native costume. It would be nice to know just what entrancing gifts were found by his excited family in the baggage

87

Hart unpacked when he reached his Newcastle home again. Among them, at any rate, were the First Grand Prize for his Canadian-made machinery, two Grand Gold Medals, and the order from Emperor Napoleon III for other Massey machines, to be used exclusively henceforth on the imperial farms.

At the Antwerp Exhibition in the summer of 1885, Massey harvesting machinery was taken apart and reconstructed after transfer to the farm of the Baron de Gruben, president of the Permanent Commission for Agriculture in the Province of Antwerp. Tested on a field of oats, it won the Gold Medal "of the highest class" over all competitors. But at the Paris Universal Exposition of 1889, another spectacular field trial was to bring far more dramatic recognition to Massey products.

The Exposition itself was a magnificent success, and *Massey's Illustrated* put out a special supplement to commemorate the event. This was the exhibition for which the Eiffel Tower was constructed, receiving mixed reactions from its observers. "By some it has been called a monstrous, hideous, and shameful atrocity," said the *Illustrated*, "by others, a great, a marvellous, and a delightful piece of work."

The gate for the Eiffel Tower alone amounted to $1,300,000, and the Exposition itself attracted twenty-five million visitors, more than double the number who attended the previous one held in 1878. It was opened on Monday, May sixth, 1889, by President Carnot (who would die by an assassin's knife five years later) and closed in November, "being a record of the history of ten years of the world's art, science and industry, set forth in visible and material documents over a space of nearly 250 acres, embracing the Trocadero, the Champ de Mars, the Quays of the Seine and the vast Esplanade des Invalides." A record of human dwellings was shown in "more than thirty habitations reconstituted with the most scrupulous exactitude from the rude huts of the Troglodytes and of the Age of Bronze, the homes of the Egyptians, the Assyrians, the Hebrews, the Etruscans, the Persians, Greeks, Romans, Aztecs, etc., down

88

to the elegant Renaissance villa and the various habitations of contemporary Europe."

The Exposition had a brilliant air of fête.

Each of the three great palaces (Fine Arts, Liberal Arts and Various Industries) was surmounted by a polychrome dome where white, turquoise blue, dull reds and brilliant gold combined to form a color-scheme that was not French, not European, but rather Assyrian, and suggestive of the friezes from the palace of Artaxerxes recently discovered at Susa. The porticoes and façades, with their blue frameworks of iron pillars and cross bars, the faience friezes, their medallions and cornices of enamelled terra-cotta; the glittering glass roofs, over which floated thousands of many-colored flags, and oriflammes; the profusion of gilding and sculpture and ornamentation; the spacious gardens, dotted with various constructions and rich with trees and flowers—all these gave an impression of variety, of multiplicity of interest and of attractiveness, that was quite new.

The Massey exhibit, its machines gleaming in the "White and Gold" of the firm's display line, won admiring comment but it was by the practical performance in the field that the big triumph of the Exposition was achieved. The contest for binders held on a ten-thousand-acre farm at Noisiel, eighteen miles outside Paris, was as breathtaking and spectacular an event as a great race meeting or a final game between matched teams.

It had, as well, something of the heroic quality of all David and Goliath tales, for every contestant except the Massey Manufacturing Company had come equipped with spare machines and service staff. The Massey contestant, William F. Johnston, superintendent of the Toronto works, arrived alone, with one Toronto Light Binder drawn from stock.

The field trial, a four-day contest, began on a bright July day in gala conditions before a crowd of spectators. The field had been divided into sections of about one and a third acres, and fifteen contestants lined up for the starting signal after lots had been drawn for position. Twenty-eight experts were present to act as jury, and one of these went with each machine to mark the evenness of cutting and binding, the number of horses and assistants used, and the time taken for the whole operation.

Johnston started off alone, with no spare driver or mechanic, and only two horses to the other entrants' three or more. He was the first to come to a stop but only for thirty seconds to buckle the canvas a little more tightly, and it was his only stop. The first-half hour saw four binders drop out, one because its section of the field was judged unfit for cutting with a machine.

Johnston finished his section in sixty-six minutes—eighteen minutes ahead of his nearest competitor—and without missing a single sheaf. Some of the contestants took more than three hours.

The second day scored an even bigger success for the Massey torchbearer. Johnston took fifty-five minutes to cut his section of oats "without a stop, or missing a sheaf, or a hindrance of any kind." The runner-up needed two and a half hours and a change of horses, and the jury had taken themselves back to Paris on the night train before some of the others had finished. In a pleasantly triumphant state of mind, Johnston galloped his team back to the cheering spectators, shook hands all round and then, in a gesture he could not resist, went onto the section considered impossible to cut in the previous day's contest, and cleaned it up with no difficulty at all.

On the third day, President Carnot attended a parade of all the machines, and the Massey Binder, "profusely decorated with the tri-color," was chosen to bind the most perfectly formed sheaf for presentation to the French president. The final day's scientific test by dynanometer put the seal on the Toronto entry's superiority. It was not surprising that *Massey's Illustrated* for November, 1889, was able to announce that "France awards The Massey M'f'g Co. Toronto, A GRAND OBJECT OF ART for their self-binder because of its vastly superior work at the Great Noisiel Field Trial, being the Highest Award given for any purpose." The announcement was illustrated by a Toronto binder drawn by two caparisoned horses through an arch of triumph before massed and cheering crowds, and a Hart-like figure modestly accepting his diploma from Marianne.

The "Grand Object of Art" itself was an "elegant statue in bronze, on a marble pedestal . . . and represents a youth, the winner of a prize, running home with a rooster reclining on a palm which he holds in his right hand, whilst, with the left arm extended, he looks back with a smile of triumph on his face and snaps his fingers at the unsuccessful competitors."

But Hart was not there in person to receive it at the presentation on December eighteenth. Tragedy had struck once again, this time at the life of his youngest son, Fred Victor.

Fred had completed his second year at the University of Toronto and followed his brother Walter in September, 1889, to the Massachusetts Institute of Technology. On his way to Boston after spending the summer in continued study, he had contracted a heavy cold; but colds, to this healthy vigorous active young man, were unimportant minor disabilities that could be shaken off in a couple of days. This one was not, but Fred Victor continued to write bouncy letters home about his studies, his friends, his future plans, and nothing at all about the hacking cough that had developed. For Thanksgiving he planned to go to Lowell, Massachusetts, where Walter's brother-in-law, the Reverend W. T. Perrin, was a minister of the Methodist Church. Only the day before leaving did his alarmed friends in Boston manage to persuade him to see a doctor who, appalled at his condition, told him to get to his friends' home as soon as possible. Arriving on November twenty-seventh, he went to bed next day, Thanksgiving Day, after a haemorrhage of the lungs, and was never up again. On January second, 1890, William Van Horne, president of the Canadian Pacific Railway, lent his private car to transport the stricken boy the six hundred and sixty miles to Toronto. For four dreadful months he lingered, bearing intense suffering with undeniable courage. His sight almost gone and emaciated beyond recognition, he died at last on April seventeenth. He would have been twenty-three in May.

Fred Victor, according to the viewpoint of the observer, was either a fine example of young Christian manhood or a stuffy young prig. Perhaps the cheerfulness of his brother Charles and the gay dignity of Walter were manifested more self-consciously in their young brother. His religious principles and beliefs were driven by a strong and aggressive personality into channels that remained uncomfortably narrow up to the time of his death. "He had no young man's follies," said the minister in the funeral address. It was almost true. He had more of Hart's intolerance than his brothers, though it seems likely that the intelligence and high spirits bringing him a wide and deserved popularity would have mellowed and modified its expression as he grew older. He was an apt student of his father's religion: two nights before he died he was singing hymns with a group of young friends in his sickroom, and he had devoted much of his time to work in the city missions. But where Chester would quietly participate and Walter would gently admonish, Fred Victor charged in like a prophet of the Lord. His habit of speaking frankly about what he considered faults in his friends must have lost him a good many of them. Neither of the Massey travellers would accept wine on the world voyage, even when troubled by thirst in areas where water was unsafe to drink. But where Walter would simply not drink, youthful Fred embellished the occasion with remonstrance and rebuke. He wrote home shortly before his last illness:

Never has my Christianity been so tried as lately. Some people claim the whole earth in themselves and curse Christianity, temperance, morality . . . and almost goodness. One such is boarding here for two or three weeks . . . That old fool will sit at the head of the table and pour out such unbearable, intolerable rot about art and its influence, and curse nearly everything good . . . The first day I let him go, and the next I made up my mind to shut him up . . . He says these things . . . not to annoy me, but to impart knowledge to others . . . I plainly told him, "I am a Methodist and not ashamed to say so either." . . . He is really a crank of the worst kind. I have downed him and others admit it. I hold him in derisive contempt, and I think I have made the others despise his views too.

The public humiliation of unbelievers was regarded by this self-appointed young moral judge not as an achievement of personal triumph, but a blow for righteousness. Had more years been allowed to him, however, his perception and real desire for goodness might well have caused him to writhe a little at such memories.

Kinsale Association Library

Visitor's-Eye View

Despite personal sorrows, life for the bereaved father had to go on. Only three weeks after Fred Victor's death, one of the great trainloads of Massey-Toronto binders made a well-publicized departure from Toronto, destined for the west coast and ultimately Australia. Twenty-one freight cars "handsomely decorated," as all four Toronto papers agreed, brought to a hundred and forty-four the total number of carloads already despatched that season to foreign markets. The centre panel of each car bore an illustration of the works, and the words, "I Am Full Of Massey-Toronto Harvesting Machines. Rush Me Along, The Farmers Are Waiting. Loaded For AUSTRALIA."

Though few Massey implements had been sold abroad up to 1886, sales through the European branch office in 1890 amounted to $125,000. Sub-agencies had been set up in France, Germany, Russia and other European countries, and also in Asia Minor and in North and South Africa. The company had seven hundred agents in Canada alone, and employed seven hundred men in the Toronto works. A contemporary account in the *Manitoba Colonist* of February, 1890, gives a remarkable picture of pioneer industrial methods and equipment:

It is startling to be told that the mere insurance plan of the works costs about $100 . . . They are situate in Toronto, about a mile from the centre of the city . . . beside the Canadian Pacific and Grand Trunk railways, and the company has its own switches from these railways directly into the works.

The buildings are of solid red brick, and the office, a very fine building, is relieved by sand stone trimmings. There are three storeys and a basement, the whole giving over 60 acres of floor space, so that a visitor can have a mile walk under roof, without

94

covering the same floor twice. The whole works are lit by electricity, and the offices by gas.

Two dynamos of 40 horse power supply the 45 arc lights and a few incandescents. An electrician is necessary, for beside the lights, there are the electric fire alarm, telephone and watchman's clock systems, electric bells, telegraph, etc. Great care is taken against fire throughout the works, each alarm signal connecting with the company's fire hall, and the striking of any one of these rings the gong in the hall, strikes a light, opens the hose-house doors, and stops the clock to show the time of alarm. Six men are on constant night duty beside the 3 night watchmen, and in addition, during the day, 2 or more men in each division take special duties in case of fire. Water is supplied from hydrants with a pressure sufficient to throw five $2\frac{1}{2}$-inch streams over forty feet high, or if required one or two streams through 100 feet of hose over 100 feet high. . .

The works occupy some seven acres, of which two acres are used for storing lumber, and here stand close set piles about forty feet high, of hickory, white ash, hard maple and bass wood, the latter being chiefly used for packing cases, while the other three are for the wooden parts of the various machines.

One skilled man is kept constantly employed buying this timber in western Ontario, and as about three million feet were used last year, his duties are not light . . .

The power for the works is supplied by three engines of about 250 horse power, with four immense boilers.

The raw material is delivered directly to the works by special switches in the yard, the coal, iron and steel going directly to the furnaces, and the lumber yarded being handled by four horses and ten men, who are constantly employed at this and other work outside. The lumber is drawn by wagons into the saw shop, the horses passing in one side of the room and unloading by a simple plan, almost without stopping, and passing out the opposite side. The lumber now passes through the various saws and machines, and is assorted and piled at once upon trucks, none being allowed upon the floor, thus saving time and labor . . .

One of nine large elevators now took the visitor to the wood shop where other time-saving methods had been introduced. By the use of brads in the forms, the various pieces were also marked for the borer as they passed through the shaping machines. Both spindle-holes in the canvas-roller were bored at the same time to exact depth, and another machine sawed and rounded the canvas slats and then reversed them to drill the necessary holes.

After the wood shop, the visitor was passed on to the construction room, where he would see the wooden rims of the various wheels being bent into shape after steaming and later placed in wooden frames to set in the drying room. The report continued:

Passing on a few steps, our guide said, "I want you to see this man make a wheel," referring to a work-man, whose constant work this is. The man placed the hub in his machine, and putting the spokes in position, drove each home with two strokes of a trip hammer, and, as our guide remarked, "Now that is there to stay, for if a bad spoke were possibly put in, the hammer strikes so hard it would break the spoke." The work-man then, without removing the wheel, with his left hand drew forward a small machine, which sawed the spokes to their proper lengths and with his right hand "tenoned" them, and in one and a half minutes, the wheel was turned out. This operation alone, would certainly make the old time carriage makers' eyes stick out, and is an instance of the great reduction of cost by improved machines, for where formerly, making these wheels cost fifty cents each, it is now reduced to a fraction.

Seeing a reaper set up, inquiry found that it is one man's sole daily work to collect from the various departments the many separate parts, and form them into the complete machine, and then take them apart and return the pieces to their places. This is done to test the work of every department. None of the many pieces are numbered, and each and all are expected to interchange, and days and years of this actual constant trial have proved that rarely indeed does any piece fail to properly fill its place. . . .

All the wood work receives a coat of paint, over its whole surface, before being fitted together, and the firm uses its own standard colors, vermilion, and "Massey Olive," with dark trimmings. After drying, the machines pass from the paint shop, to the store room, thousands of square feet close packed with the various pieces, painted and ready for fitting, divided into lots, but not numbered, as every piece is expected and known to be interchangeable. One large room is devoted to packing implements for foreign countries, as the trade of this house extends pretty well round the globe.

All turpentine, oils, or dangerous materials are stored under ground, and apart from the main building, so that their explosion could not destroy the works. Here is a tank for turpentine, and it holds just a car load, and here, also, are tiers of barrels of white lead, of which a ton is used every 4 or 5 days.

The various parts of the binder gathered from the various sections, to the fitting up room, and growing in semblance, are finally taken hold of by the finisher, who tests them by accurate work, though broom corn takes the place of grain in the binding test. . . .

The knives for the cutter bars are of the finest steel, which comes in long thin sheets, whose width is sufficient to allow the die to cut a "section" or knife from each side, leaving very little waste. The sections are then placed in trays and evened, several dozen at a time, they are then packed in other trays, and tempered in an oven, to an absolute equality, and they are then bored, counter-sunk, riveted, faced and bevelled.

Seeing some cars holding grindstones at one of the companies switches, we found they were used in this department. They are six feet in diameter, and twelve inches thick, and yet one of them only lasts a week, and seven are generally in use at once, which will give some idea of the extent of the work. All the smoke and dust from these shops is gathered by exhaust fans, and blown into the chimneys.

The wrought iron is taken from the cars under shelter, loaded upon trolleys and the various sizes passed to the shears, which can cut a bar of steel four inches by three-quarter inch, as a man would munch a soda biscuit. In the blacksmith shop the drop-forging at once attracts attention, for here at one blow the metal is in a moment put in a certain shape at a cost five times less than in former years. . . .

Hart Massey's forward-looking methods led him to close observation of invention and progress everywhere. He would buy any new gadget he saw and pass it to his experts for testing and experimentation. A whole building was devoted to pattern making, and in this he kept samples of machines made by his competitors as well as his own early models, against which the innovations of later years were tested. The *Manitoba Colonist* went on:

The tool room is an important place, as all the tools used in this factory are made on the premises. Here in a room 20 by 40 feet, with blacksmith shop attached, eight skilled men are constantly employed in this work, aided by improved and costly machinery.

97

Where so many men use such numbers of varied tools many of them expensive, an effective delivery check is necessary. This is had by storing the tools in separate boxes, with a corresponding frame of numbered hooks. A workman desiring a certain tool, rings the bell at the wicket of the tool room. If it is an exchange he hands in the worn tool to the attendant and if a common tool it is thrown into a box, and repaired when sufficient have been gathered, and a fresh one is given him. If a more expensive tool is needed, a check bearing its name is hung upon the hook with the same number as the man, it can be thus seen exactly how many tools are out, what kind, and who is using them.

There are some still more expensive tools, and in getting these the workman deposits a brass check, which is put in the place of the tool received and is returned on delivery of the tool. In paying off men who are ceasing work they must be square with the tool room. It is very important that an exact check shall be kept upon the men's time, where so many hundreds are employed. Therefore on the wall of the Superintendent's office is a self registering dial connected with the turnstile outside, through which all the workmen enter, and which is held against him if desired, by a lever under the foot of the checking clerk inside, a glass wicket giving a view of the stile.

Each man is supplied with a numbered check bearing the firm's initials, which in passing he drops into a slot, and it falls in front of the clerk, and he cannot enter until this is so dropped. These checks are filed on boards holding from 20 to 60 each, corresponding with the sections of the works in which the men are engaged, and shortly before ceasing hours, these boards are carried to the foreman, who delivers them to the men, who at the proper time pour out through the great main doors of the building. Should a man wish to leave before regular hours, he gets from his foreman an order on the office for his time check, and by it can pass out through the turnstile. As no man can enter the works except by the turnstile, or leave it except by the main entrance doors, it follows that he cannot receive pay for more time than he puts in, or leave or enter unknown to the officers. This office also has perfect speaking connections by either tube or telephone with all the 23 foremen while in their respective divisions, and they can likewise talk with the office.

Every Saturday night the Superintendent receives from each foreman, a report of the total work in each division, during the week, upon printed forms, a different color being used for each division. By these the Superintendent can tell in a few minutes, without leaving the office, what has been done and whether the supplies are sufficient, and can increase or decrease the output of any department at once by telephone order. For one instance, take the finished work report for the wood shop for the week ending Nov. 9th, '89, on a form headed: Toronto Light Binder, No. 3 A, this being a well known machine. Here are 80 articles specified, and of these we find there were made that week 10,662 "reel-fan arms," and 365 "main wheel rims." Now as the latter number is too low to keep up with the work going on in other divisions, the Superintendent would at once call the attention of the foreman of that division, find the reason and increase the output. A great saving of time, and exactness in tracing these things, is shown by this very plan. . . .

The figures of the principal supplies will give an idea of the quantity of raw material used. The list includes five kinds of iron, ten kinds of steel, three of wire, two of springs and two kinds of brass, also copper, zinc and lead, several varieties of wood, hard and soft, also hard coal and soft coal, coke, three grades of bolts, with nuts, washers, rivets, burrs, nails, tacks and screws. There are three kinds of sand, with fire clay, resin, pot ash and chalk. Then come leather in various forms, saws, drills, grindstones, and various working tools, besides emery paper, brushes of several kinds, cord, and cotton duck. There are no less than ten kinds of oil, with white lead, red lead and varnishes. Among the odd things are brooms, molasses, walrus-hide, beeswax, bones, flour and window glass. Though they may seem small or out of place, yet in the moulding shop, about twenty barrels of flour were used last year and a large amount of molasses, while over three tons of bones were used in the case hardening department, and in sweeping the floors about 200 specially made brooms were worn out. The visitor would scarcely think that broken glass formed much of an item in this factory, but every autumn it is one man's business to replace these, and it just required 1,000 odd lights for those broken during the past year. . . .

"Upon the fortieth anniversary," concluded the report, "the Company's output had reached a total of 100,000 machines, the annual product having increased from fifty to ten thousand."

It should be remembered that at this time only a decade had passed since Thomas Edison had evolved a workable electric lighting system, and that another decade was to pass before Henry Ford would develop the rudiments of true mass production.

A Massey event was the annual "Pic-Nic," with special trains to take the picnickers to Niagara or Newcastle.

For the fortieth anniversary of the company in 1887 a big family picnic to Newcastle was organized with the usual Massey attention for detail. Each worker received a printed programme giving exact times of all events, from 7.20 A.M. when "Both Trains leave Toronto" to 9.15 P.M., "Arrival home." Baggage cars were provided for baby carriages and lunch baskets (to be labelled with the owners' names) and the first car of the first train was reserved for members of the band and their families. Fourteen hundred men, women and children spent the day at Newcastle (by 1898 the number would have swollen to three thousand five hundred and require six special trains). The villagers flocked to meet the train, and "to the music of the band the excursionists paraded through the town's streets, which had been strung with flags and mottoes expressing the welcome of the townspeople. Arrived at the grove, the young men and women at once turned their attention to the amusements which had been provided, whilst the older ones who had lived originally in Newcastle were greeting their former friends."

Swings, quoit-pitching, baseball, swimming and a band concert preceded the schedule of games, the baby show and the "most popular lady" contest (the lady won a parlour suite of furniture worth $100). There was a wide range of prizes for the games: "Organette, $8; Ham and Shirt, $2.50; 1 doz. spoons, $2.50; Sewing Machine, $15; Pants and 1 year's subscription to *Labour Reformer*, $3.50; Half Ton Coal, $3.25; Bread Tickets, $1.00."

At the picnic, Hart and Eliza were presented with an illuminated address and a "piece of porcelain." By a happy coincidence, 1887 was also the fortieth anniversary of their wedding.

Toward the end of 1890, Hart was in England to bring himself up to date on certain business developments. Competition

100

from other Canadian implement manufacturers, notably A. Harris Son and Company of Brantford, was offering a serious threat to Massey supremacy. Though the spectacular success of the Harris Brantford Open-End Binder in 1890 could probably have been duplicated by a Massey version incorporating the same principles of operation, a different choice was made, and amalgamation of the two firms under the name the Massey-Harris Company Limited was announced to a surprised world on May sixth, 1891. This was followed in December by what *Massey's Illustrated* reported as "a wedding," in which the Patterson-Wisner Company joined with Massey-Harris. "While the bride, as is usual, has sacrificed her maiden name, all the good will which attached to it accrues to the bridegroom, and Massey-Harris Co. Ltd. boasts of having wedded into a good family." A percentage interest in various other firms making related implements gave the company a full line of agricultural machinery, which offered many advantages to employee and purchaser alike. The company was now the largest of its kind in the British Empire.

From Music Hall to Mission Centre

By the time he died in 1896, Hart Massey had earned a reputation as a public benefactor. Always generous with donations to causes he believed in (the Newcastle Methodist parsonage, in 1847, was one of the first), Hart had made his first substantial gift when he endowed a chair of Religious Education at Victoria College, and various departments of the Methodist Church, including the Chautauqua Assembly, New York, of which he was an early trustee, had had cause over the years to rejoice in his benevolence. In the latter part of his life, when he was established as a person of civic importance and responsibility, his generous impulses spread over a wider area. Two of his biggest gifts to the people of Toronto, totalling between them more than $210,000, were opened in 1894: the Massey Music Hall on June fourteenth, in memory of Charles Albert, his eldest son, and on October twenty-fifth the Fred Victor Mission, in memory of his youngest.

The Massey Music Hall would give to Toronto a centre for cultural life whose value it is hard to overestimate. The suggestion for a hall where good music could be heard at a reasonable price under the best conditions probably originated with F. H. Torrington, organist at the Metropolitan Church and a leader in the Toronto musical world, who had had the honour of playing the organ in St. Patrick's Church, Montreal, at the funeral of D'Arcy McGee in 1868. Up to that time, concerts had been held in a variety of buildings, notably the too-small and unsuitable Horticultural Pavilion in Allan Gardens. "What Toronto needs," Mr. Torrington remarked one day to Hart Massey, "is a good music hall."

Hart made a noncommittal reply but the seed took root, and in his decisive way the old man went into action. He invited his sons Chester and Walter and their wives to discuss the proposal, at his home rather than at Walter's because Eliza Ann was reluctant to cross Jarvis Street on account of the heavy traffic: "the bicycles were an awful nuisance." He then invited Mr. Torrington to join them at dinner in the dining-room with the big bay window and the massive built-in mahogany sideboard that almost filled one wall.

"What," he asked the astounded organist, "do you think of the corner of Shuter and Victoria streets as a site for a music hall?"

When the plan was announced the public rushed into print with comment and advice. The city council was not enthusiastic about the proposal and refused Hart's request for municipal tax exemption on the grounds that the city had no share in its management. The *Weekly Times* was not sure that it approved a gift for Toronto. "How many reapers and threshing machines did Toronto citizens ever buy from him," it asked pointedly, "at protection prices? In his commendable efforts to get rid of his wealth, Mr. Massey should not forget other communities which have contributed far more than Toronto to his pile." "Agricola" wanted an agricultural hall instead. "Respectable Size," who had wriggled uncomfortably in too-narrow seats and anticipated that North Americans of future generations would become bigger, asked the architects to make sure of good spacing between seats. One correspondent demanded a bathing establishment for men, women and children, complete with gymnasium and Turkish baths. Suggestions poured in for a winter garden with tropical plants; parks and playing fields; a cultural centre with a small gallery and rooms for Thespians, biologists, astronomers and writers; and (with heavy sarcasm) a few poorhouses to accommodate downtrodden Massey employees.

The gift of the Music Hall (the modifier was formally dropped in 1933 after the term "music hall" had developed another connotation) was unique in a day when most benefactors thought in terms of hospitals and religious buildings. But the Masseys were all lovers of music, and Hart's intention was to provide a building easily accessible to the people of Toronto, then numbering just under 185,000, where "musical, educational or other entertainments of the highest class" would be made available to the greatest number of people at the lowest possible cost.

The building, erected in 1894, remains essentially the same today, with the addition of an area at the back not then available to Hart Massey and since converted to office and dressing-room space and enlargement of the stage. The external measurements were 122 feet by 132 feet. There were just over thirteen hundred seats on the ground floor, and almost two thousand on the balcony and gallery that, supported by slender pillars, ran around three sides of the building. Behind the stage, until they were removed fifteen years later, three hundred more seats rose in tiers to accommodate the large choirs, which were a feature of that day and later and which reached a high standard of performance: the Mendelssohn Choir, the National Chorus, the Oratorio Society, the People's Choral Union, the Orpheus Society, the Toronto Male Chorus, the Women's Musical Club and the thousand child voices of the massed school choirs.

Though today's sophisticated taste gives amused toleration to the ornate Moorish architecture, something in the design and construction of Massey Hall has endowed it with a superb acoustical quality. Rated sixth on the list of the world's concert halls, it was elevated to second place—ahead of the Vienna Opera House—when Dr. Fritz Winckel, acoustical authority and professor at West Berlin's Technical University, visited Massey Hall in 1961, shooting off blank cartridges down the aisle and exclaiming "Ah!" in delighted approbation. "Pistol Packin' Professor Partial to Massey Hall," said the *Globe and*

Mail in a burst of alliteration. "Don't meddle with this hall," said the professor emphatically, "Don't change a thing— even if it looks antique."

Whether by expert knowledge or by mere happy chance, elements in the blank curved wall at the back of the stage or the scalloped Moorish arch overhead or the pendentives spaced at intervals along the ceiling and continuing the Moorish theme have enabled choirs, orchestras, solo musicians and speakers to be heard by their audiences to the best possible advantage. No less a person than Lloyd George would comment within its walls on the ease with which a speaker could be heard, and seventy years after its opening Canadian soprano Lois Marshall wrote, out of experience in several hundred different halls around the world, "For music generally and singing in particular, I would put Massey Hall among the first six for helping to make the artist's life a joyous and rewarding one. This is not only my feeling. I have spoken to countless singers and instrumentalists who have appeared in Massey Hall, and they have all mentioned their unforgettable pleasure in performing there."

The first performance of a three-day music festival officially opened the hall on June fourteenth, 1894. From the Massey box, the middle of three one above the other on the right of the stage and later to be used for broadcasting purposes, seven-year-old Vincent watched the stooped, grey-bearded figure of his grandfather appear to greet the audience, supported by two tall sons. Among the performers was pianist Arthur Friedheim, a favourite pupil of Liszt, and the Grand Festival Choir was directed by Mr. Torrington, who was to direct the Philharmonic Choir and Orchestra until 1912 (he died in 1917).

Massey Hall, which cost Hart a precise total of $152,390.75, contained the most modern equipment available at the time, including a ventilating and cooling system to change the air every five minutes, and the largest chandelier ever made by a New York firm. Later, by the sacrifice of several seats, a smoking lounge was added at the rear of the balcony, and—giving up still more accommodation—the ground-floor seats were better spaced for comfort ("Respectable Size" at last having proved his point). The first staircases were narrow, steep, wooden affairs. Today, like the new floor that has replaced the original, they are of steel and concrete, wide, shallow and functional.

Three hundred and fifty-seven thousand patrons attended Massey Hall events in the first year of its existence, to hear musicians and lecturers and religious leaders at sixty-five daytime and a hundred and twenty-eight evening engagements. At one of Dwight Moody's religious revival meetings the evangelist paid a public tribute to the donor from the platform.

But though the events were popular, the financial difficulties of the hall were considerable in the first few years. Hart Massey had instructed that the surplus he confidently expected should be put first to repairs and improvements, next to building up a fund for emergency expenses, and finally to lowering the price of admission. His main purpose, to bring good entertainment within the reach of everyone, was expressed practically in a large block of seats in the top gallery reserved for students and other impecunious music-lovers. But during the years of national depression that followed its opening, the hall had to continue meeting city taxes and could not, under the terms of the trust deed, be mortgaged. Over the years, too, fire safety regulations became more stringent, and any surplus was usually spent on bigger and better fire escapes spider-webbing up the outer walls.

There was provision for the disposal of the building if the trustees foresaw a lasting deficiency and the expenses should heavily outbalance the income, in which case the money realized from the sale was to go to suitable charities. But assistance to cover deficits came from other members of the family from time to time and by 1900, with returning national prosperity and a more vigorous policy by members of the Massey Hall board, the problem no longer existed.

The large seating capacity meant that admission prices could be lowered whenever New York managers did not insist

106

on the same admission scale as in American cities. But at whatever price, Massey Hall was a godsend to the cultural life of Torontonians, who could now hear people with world-famous names on their own doorstep, so to speak.

The roster of performers and personalities who came to Massey Hall over the years reads like a volume of *Who's Who*. The La Scala orchestra came from Milan in 1906 with Leoncavallo, in 1920 with Toscanini. Mascagni brought his Italian Opera Company, Leopold Stokowski his Philadelphia Orchestra, Victor Herbert the Pittsburgh Symphony Orchestra. Jascha Heifetz and Mischa Elman were each seventeen when they first appeared on the Massey Hall stage; Yehudi Menuhin and Fritz Kreisler have also been guest violinists. Paderewski, Rachmaninoff, and Toronto's own Hambourg brothers, Mark, Jan and Boris, made several appearances, also de Pachmann, whose playing of Chopin at the age of seventy was likened to "pearls on velvet—hot pearls," in 1925.

For one performance in 1911 the Imperial Russian Ballet visited Toronto "by consent of His Imperial Majesty The Czar," when the programmes bore the double-headed eagle, crest of the Emperor of All the Russias. An exhibition of ballroom dancing by Irene and Vernon Castle contrasted with the passionate beauty of Anna Pavlova in ballet.

The great voices of Lotte Lehmann, Ernestine Schumann-Heink, Dame Nellie Melba, Adelina Patti (she was sixty when the audience took her to its heart in 1903), the Irish tenor John McCormack and Edward Johnson, later to become father-in-law to Conservative leader George Drew, all have echoed in the ears of enchanted Toronto listeners. The Russian singer Chaliapin, who had a bit part in *The Barber of Seville* in 1926, sang solo to a packed house ten years later. Enrico Caruso gave his first Toronto concert in 1908.

"There was really no mistaking the audience's appreciation of Caruso," the *Toronto Star* reported next day. "When handclapping failed to express its emotions, it resorted to cheers, and even then it may be safely hazarded it had its enthusiasm under restraint, for it is just possible that it stood a little in awe of the 'greatest tenor of a century.' " The greatest tenor gave encores to all his numbers, and remarked "I like very much the city of Toronto."

Other voices, could some kind of time machine pick them out of the silent past, would still stir their hearers. Sir Arthur Conan Doyle, Sir Oliver Lodge and Bertrand Russell, Hilaire Belloc and Pierre van Paassen; Clarence Darrow; Winston Churchill telling of his Boer War experiences, and Helen Keller bravely forcing a voice she could never hear herself; the three Pankhursts, Emmeline, Sylvia and Christabel, and Canada's Emily Stowe-Gullen, urging the rights of women to the vote; Peary, Shackleton, Amundsen, in heroic stories of Arctic and Antarctic adventure; Ellen Terry's enchanting voice talking about the heroines of Shakespeare.

Religious fervour, too, has stirred in the enclosed air. Here Gypsy Smith, the Methodist evangelist, thundered his warnings of hellfire, and the Christian Scientists, the British Israelites and the Oxford Group expounded their views to Sunday gatherings. The Salvation Army leaders, William Booth and his daughter Evangeline, have here addressed their followers, and here (Hart would have been pleased) a Massey grandson, Walter's son Denton, closed the 1929 season of his York Bible Class in a crowded Massey Hall.

An early performance that attracted a full house (though most of the audience departed when the main event was over and a programme of songs began) was the bayonet match just before Christmas in 1897, when two champions of the art preceded the bout with a dramatic demonstration of sword-cutting, chopping a potato without harming the handkerchief in which it was wrapped, and slicing lead bars, sheets of paper and ribbons. In November, 1919, the hall reverberated with thunderous denunciations of vaccination, during which the mayor was hissed, the "slaughter of innocent children" deplored and "another big war" was foretold "if you are going to force people to have their bodies mutilated."

Both death and marriage have found a place within the hall. Here the Honourable John Beverley Robinson died in 1896 during a meeting conducted by Sir Charles Tupper, and here Tom Longboat, Indian marathon runner, was married to Miss F. Maracle in 1908. In 1900, flickering biograph movies showed Canadian Boer War volunteers marching down Yonge Street, and the first motion picture of Canadian soldiers in action was shown in Massey Hall early in 1915. For one performance, *The Merchant of Venice* was played in Yiddish. A mass meeting in 1912 discussed the perennial subject of public morals. In April of the same year a grieving congregation, heads bowed in shock and sorrow, prayed for the victims of the *Titanic* in "last Monday morning's disaster."

As well, Massey Hall has seen stranger activities than all of these, and some that would surely have astonished—and perhaps perturbed—the donor. Would he have approved the wrestling bouts and boxing matches—even with Jack Dempsey? Or Isadora Duncan, dancing to Gluck's *Iphigenia in Aulis*, even though the Toronto *Mail* said afterwards, "She appears with bare limbs and diaphanous draperies but her dances are presented with an illusion so charming that they body forth dreamland rather than suggest anything fleshy"? He would have liked the meetings that vocally disapproved the introduction of Sunday street cars, but while he might have sympathized with the citizens who came to protest pay-as-you-enter cars, he would certainly have frowned when they poured out of the hall to break all the streetcar windows within reach.

Yet it is with music that Massey Hall has always been chiefly concerned, whether of choir or solo, band or orchestra. The Toronto Symphony Orchestra, so closely associated with Massey Hall, was organized in 1907 as the Toronto Conservatory

Symphony Orchestra and came to full flower in 1931 under Dr. (later Sir) Ernest MacMillan, aided by a devoted auxiliary of Toronto men and women.

As recently as June, 1965, Herbert Whittaker of the *Globe and Mail* called Massey Hall "that irreplaceable musical shrine." Hart Massey gave his eldest son a better memorial than he knew —not a building only, but an enriched and expanding cultural life for the people of his city.

The Fred Victor Mission, Hart's memorial to his other dead son, had had its origin in the work of Mrs. M. T. Sheffield, a devoted member of the Metropolitan Church. Her interest in "the waifs of the street" had led to a Sunday class in 1886, held in a room in the Orange Hall, to whose first and second meetings no one came. Mrs. Sheffield knelt alone and prayed "that the room might be the birthplace of souls and where a new direction might be given to many lives." On the third Sunday, four little boys left the game of marbles they had been playing at the door and came upstairs, parking their chewing tobacco in their pockets for later use. They liked the singing, the Bible stories. Next Sunday they brought three friends, sternly policing them for removal of their "quids" while in class.

The mission had four locations and quite a few difficulties before it moved into the grand building that Hart Massey donated. The class numbered twenty street boys in the old frame building on Church Street, though the ringing of the fire bells would empty the room in a twinkling of its entire audience. The mission's next home, in a Lombard Street basement, was opposite a notorious lodging house, and its class members were distinctly annoyed by an invasion of the derelict lodgers. A mission lodging house on Jarvis Street began a more aggressive work among tramps, drunkards and homeless men, and a few women and girls began to trickle in for the mothers' meetings and sewing classes held along with gospel classes, night schools, gymnasium, an employment bureau and other agencies. The young Fred Victor

110

used to spend time working at these early locations, and play his flute with obtuse sincerity to entertain the less fortunate.

The grand opening of the Fred Victor Mission, which cost Hart $60,000, was held on October twenty-sixth, 1894. A pleasing bronzed brick had been used for the upper three of its five storeys, and the interior had been specially equipped for its purpose. One third of its space was designed for the lodging house, with bathrooms, reading- and smoking-rooms, and accommodation for two hundred and twenty-six men. A mission hall seated five hundred. Separate quarters were provided for a restaurant and a "baby shelter," a manual training area, an employment bureau, a boys' gymnasium with bath and dressing-rooms, class rooms and even a "drunk's room," where a client could "dry out" before being accepted at the lodging house. The forty-seven rooms had been built to meet the needs of the day but with an eye to the future, and many offshoots of the mission's concern for human distress had their origin here. The Victor Five-Cent Savings Association begun in 1892 became the Penny Bank of Ontario, operated throughout the public school system. The Victor Kindling Wood Company working from Victor Inn, an old hotel on King Street, was started here in 1907. The Victor Home for Unmarried Mothers arose out of the time a woman came to the Fred Victor Mission needing medical help. The "Kitchen Garden" classes started by Emily Huntingdon to teach little girls from underprivileged homes that orderly housework could be pleasurable grew into the domestic science classes in which Hart's daughter Lillian was to take such devoted and practical interest.

There had been a real estate boom around Toronto in 1889, which had encouraged people to foresee a magnificent Metropolitan Toronto, a series of neat little satellites all taking pride in the central city of their origin. A steam railway, the Belt Line, would serve the satellites; plans were drawn up and enough track laid for several trial runs to emphasize Toronto's future greatness. But the boom petered out. Everyone was poor, and in 1890 conditions were so bad that a rush of slum missions sprang up,

111

doing what they could to alleviate the troubles of the body as well as of the soul. Liquor was cheap and uncontrolled, whisky five cents a glass, beer five cents a tankard, an easy escape from the vice and poverty that flourished. Men chewed their tobacco instead of smoking it: a "chaw" could fool the appetite, for a while anyway.

Some of the missions were inferior places of bad food and disease, full of refugees from the police doubling up two to a bed, and the lodgers got more gospel than groceries. Yet they did their best with unpaid workers and superintendents who themselves earned little more than a dollar a day and accommodation for their families. The Fred Victor Mission made an earnest attempt to alleviate conditions and raise the status of the indigent by kind and decent treatment. A man could get twenty-one meals and seven sleeping places a week for $2.70 and, if he could afford it, a separate bed for fifteen cents a night. The men slept twelve in a room, in six double-decker iron beds, for ten cents a night. Good simple meals cost ten cents, and second-hand clothing was often available. "The Mission was a fine generous gesture," comments an eighty-five-year-old Torontonian who knew the city of those days, "but it was misinterpreted at the time as another example of Massey ostentation."

Not too many years later, B. K. Sandwell would write, "Toronto has no social classes/Only the Masseys and the masses."

On February twentieth, 1896—it happened to be the ninth birthday of his grandson Vincent—the news came of Hart Massey's death at seventy-three during the singing of Haydn's *The Creation* in Massey Hall by Torrington's choir. The lights in the Massey box were put out and the curtains drawn. "At the conclusion of the splendid oratorio," reported the Toronto *Globe* next day, "the conductor, in brief but fitting terms, announced that the builder of the hall was no more, and the entire assemblage rose as the great organ pealed forth in the most effective manner Handel's 'Dead March in Saul.' " Two of his sisters survived him.

The youngest, Alida, had married an Englishman, William Watts, and lived in Settle, Yorkshire. The eldest, Elvira Powell, lived until November, 1904, and celebrated with her husband, who died in March that year, her sixty-second wedding anniversary.

The Prime Minister of Canada, Sir Mackenzie Bowell, came to attend the simple ceremony in the Jarvis Street house. A choral service followed in Metropolitan Church, and thousands lined the streets to see the funeral cortège, three-quarters of a mile long, that accompanied the old pioneer to his resting place in the ponderous mausoleum he had built in 1894 in Mount Pleasant cemetery. ("I'd rather have a yacht," irrepressible Walter had said.)

Toronto would miss Hart Massey in many ways. His family would recall him with mixed feelings. His wife had lost a strong and gentle husband. His sons, who had earned his respect, were now bereft of shrewd and companionable advice in the conduct of the firm's business. His only daughter would remain torn between love and resentment, appreciating his lavish generosity, knowing that his feeling for her had amounted almost to idolatry but knowing, too, that his restrictions on her social life had kept her unmarried long past the time for romance. His grandchildren would always remember the big grey-bearded man who huffed at them with twinkling eyes, but whose displeasure could petrify. Seventy-odd years later, Vincent could still give a reminiscent shudder, recalling the small boy who had had to face his grandfather after an irate gardener had caught him with a bunch of pilfered grapes.

The older grandchildren who visited from time to time also occasionally ran into grandfather's sterner aspect. Once Charley's spirited daughter Jennie (she liked to call herself Jane) on vacation from the Ontario Ladies College at Whitby was caught at dusk talking to a boy over the garden gate. Hauled inside and lectured on the disgraceful episode, she spent two days on bread and water, while Bertie and Bessie smuggled food to her up the

113

Kinsale Association Library

back stairs ("and I think grandfather was well aware of it," Bessie remarked some seventy years later), after which she was banished to her great-aunt Elvira's farm in Cobourg for the rest of the summer. Since she had always loved animals, this was no punishment.

A reporter would remember the Massey president as the energetic driver of a two-horse mower in a Dominion Day parade, who threw down a quarter as he galloped past and called with a wink, "Give me a good write-up!"

A shivering newsboy, fifteen minutes late with the morning paper, would cower at the memory of a terrifying figure in dressing gown and slippers standing on the front doormat, watch in hand at 6 A.M., thundering reprimands. He would also not forget the gruff "What for?" that acknowledged his own stammered thanks next morning for a complete winter outfit delivered within hours by the Massey coachman.

There was the story that told how Hart, awaiting a visit from the general manager of the Bank of Commerce, Mr. (later Sir Edmund) Walker, from whom he was seeking a loan, placed men in strategic locations along King Street to signal his approach. As his carriage drew near the works, Hart, in shirtsleeves, could be seen busily ploughing a strip of ground beneath the office windows. When the visitor had arrived, he bustled into the office, dusting off his hands, and gave a well-feigned start on seeing Mr. Walker.

"Just testing a plough," he said nonchalantly. "Never let a piece go out without my personal inspection." The impressed banker, the story goes, granted the loan.

Some of the anecdotes have become larger-than-life-size over the years. Certainly the old man was credited with eagle-eyed observation and a persistent preoccupation with penny-pinching. It was said that he could spot a spoiled nail at a hundred feet, and an unlikely story is still repeated about the time he roared, "Dock that workman for wasted material," when a luckless employee fell into a vat of red paint. When an employee lost a

114

leg in an elevator accident, Hart ordered that he should have a job with the company as long as he lived. And he respected a man who would stand up to him. He had nothing but a twinkle for the elevator operator who carried him past the floor he wanted and met his reprimand with a grumpy, "What do you expect, a mind-reader for a dollar a day?"

With wry humour in those days of low wages and harsh discipline, Hart's workmen would tell another story about the man in the asylum next door who had had his brains removed for repair and didn't bother to go back for them when he was made a Massey-Harris foreman. "Don't need brains to take a job like that," he explained. In days when labour was still struggling to organize and protect itself against management's ruthlessness a job at twelve dollars a week was a princely wage, and the foremen were slave-drivers who hired and fired, who filled the shops with men of their own creed and race, on whose order to shovel snow from a private walk might depend a man's job. Though there were girls in a Toronto glove factory who would remember that Hart Massey publicly championed their cause in a strike, many of his own striking workmen on other occasions would regard this as a bitter joke. The Methodist conscience that led Hart to good works and paternalism saw no anomaly in wage-cutting during periods of depression.

The will Hart left to dispose of his estate of almost two million dollars has been called a remarkable document for its (up to that time) almost unparalleled public generosity. Not only was it spelled out to cover every contingency and every plan the old man had for each beneficiary but the larger part of it was left, not to his family (though all of them, down to specifically named children of his wife's relatives, were more than adequately cared for) but to charitable, educational and cultural causes. An ample allowance would permit Eliza Ann to maintain and enjoy the family residence. After her death, Lillian would get "all the silverware, table furniture, crockery and general table outfits;

115

bric-à-brac in connection with the cabinet; parlor furniture, house-hold linen and bedding": the balance, including "household furniture and other appurtenances . . . the barn and stable furniture, carriages, buggies and wagons, horses and harness, robes and other equipments and utensils," would go in equal shares to all three children.

For granddaughter Winona Grace, the "little miss" whose birth had brightened an early Christmas in Cleveland, there was strict justice and a warning. Winnie had grown into a beautiful girl whose dark hair glinted with gold lights and whose gaiety and charm are still remembered by nephews and nieces today. Her matrimonial troubles had disturbed her grandfather. "I had built a home on St. George Street, Toronto," Hart said from the grave, "for my granddaughter Winona Grace Watson, which cost me something over eight thousand dollars, and which home was occupied for some time by my said granddaughter and her husband, but as they could not agree to live together my said granddaughter left said home and desired me to sell the same, which I did, and I received the proceeds from the sale of the house and property . . . which I have directed to be invested for her benefit during her lifetime." This amount was to be deducted from her fifth-share of the $75,000 bequeathed to the children of Hart's eldest son Charles Albert, and the remainder invested for Winnie's benefit. The executors were directed, however, not to make payment to her of any of the interest "until in their sole and absolute discretion it is by reason of her general good conduct and also her manner and treatment of them and my family . . . deemed proper and expedient."

The bequest to Charles Albert's family was the subject of a lawsuit, finally settled out of court, that caused a rift in family relations for many years afterwards. Sixteen-year-old Bessie, visiting from school, was aware of whisperings among the adults abruptly shut off at her approach. When her grandmother brought the subject up on one occasion, Bessie, wise beyond her years, remarked that she could not comment without further

116

knowledge of what was going on. The younger generation of today, far removed from the bitterness of those days, is inclined to regard it all as something of a joke.

Hart's will provided for other sums varying from $200,000 down to $1,000 to a long list of beneficiaries, from Victoria College, Toronto, and Mount Allison College, Sackville, New Brunswick, to the Salvation Army, the Upper Canada Tract Society, the Toronto Home for Incurables, the National Sanitarium Association and "worn-out and needy [Methodist] ministers." The remainder was left equally to Chester, Lillian and Walter.

Fairs and a Fez

For the first two or three years of their marriage Walter Massey and his young bride Susan Denton had lived at Euclid Hall, as the Jarvis Street house had been rather pretentiously named. In 1890, with their year-old daughter Ruth, they moved to 486 Jarvis, a compact stone-fronted house almost directly across the road. Susan's quiet dignity had endeared her to the whole family, especially Hart, who had strongly approved of her punctuality at the breakfast table. Lilly dawdled over dressing and was often late. On more than one occasion the coachman had to drive the restive horses out onto the street and round the semicircular drive to the front entrance a couple of times before Lillian was ready to come downstairs.

✳ Little Ruth and her cousin Vincent, two years older, who lived with his father Chester and mother Anna Vincent in the house next door to grandfather's, were like sister and brother, bringing back to the big house the joyous childish frolics Hart had enjoyed with Bessie and Bertie. They, too, stared at the goldfish, watched the landau on its wash-rack being hosed down by the coachman, were enthralled by the curious treasures brought home by their world-travelling uncles. There were no longer any antic monkeys to laugh at nor an Uncle Fred whose trilling on the flute filled early morning and late night hours, and they were too young to have seen the merry sleighing parties, when uncles and aunts and older cousins (teen-aged Winnie, Jennie and Arthur) would go off on a farm wagon into the open country north of Bloor Street and down the wild Rosedale ravines. But they were warmed by the same love from their grandfather, creating a private world of fantasy for themselves among the

118

Vinona Grace (Winnie) Massey

Bessie Irene and Charles Albert II, Charles Albert Massey's two youngest children

Valter and Susan Massey, with Madeline, Ruth and Dorothy, 1888/89

*Hart Almerrin Massey with his grand-
children Vincent Massey and Ruth Massey*

Raymond Massey, aged about five

Ruth, Dorothy, Mrs. Hart Massey and Denton Massey

Massey Hall, with (centre) the Massey box

Looking out to the patio at "Susan's Folly"

Vincent and Raymond Massey, 1964

Denton Massey, 1964

PHOTO BY "CHATELAINE" MAGAZI
NORMUNDS BERZI

Massey College

PHOTO BY R. J. THOM, PARTNER-IN-CHI
THOMPSON, BERWICK, PRATT & PARTNE

shrubs and bushes of his shaggy garden or dressing up in wonderful costumes from the big box in the attic. The few quarrels between the two children sent them both into ostentatious mourning, Ruth with a black bow in her hair, Vincent wearing a black cravat.

"Vincent and I were almost spoiled as grandchildren," Ruth remembered in a CBC broadcast in 1961. "I think Grandfather Massey liked us both pretty much. We used to have a great many family parties and Vincent and I were always taken in on these parties. We used to sit through long dinners and wait for the ice-cream and then we were excused."

They played indoors in the attic, full of all sorts of things. "I remember the old engravings, the nineteenth-century engraving of the end of the world. We were not allowed to ride our bicycles on Sunday. We played quite freely with other children in the neighbourhood, but we were also a continual source of entertainment to ourselves."

The children went to church and Sunday school, and after a family supper everyone would join in singing hymns. "We were really very devoted," Ruth said. At her funeral, after her death in 1962 at the age of seventy-two, Vincent was visibly upset.

It was Vincent who turned the first sod and, later, six-and-a-half and in his Sunday-best sailor suit, laid the foundation stone of Massey Hall on September twenty-first, 1893. The ceremony was the first of many similar performances. Years later, in the gorgeous dignity of a chancellor's robes, Vincent Massey would lay the foundation stone of the Sir Daniel Wilson Residence at the University of Toronto with such careful precision that a bystander muttered, "I wonder if he has his union card?"

Ruth's father, Walter, with characteristic enterprise, had acquired a camp property on Sparrow Lake in the Muskoka district of Ontario. An outsize muskellunge lurking beneath the lake waters posed a challenge he could not resist. He caught the monster after some years of trying but not before he had been

119

neatly fooled by his older brother Chester, a confirmed practical joker, whose excited cries for help in landing his catch one night brought Walter, in pyjamas, hurriedly from his tent. When the furore had died down, Walter found that what he had caught was not the muskellunge but a dead and gutted thirty-pound salmon.

At the camp the whole family spent weeks of summer fun, living in rough frame cottages or in tents. Susan disliked tenting and hated the thunderstorms that swept across the hills. But the children spent excitingly different days, fishing, boating, rambling in the woods, picking blueberries, Bessie (who dearly loved her grandfather despite the earlier family rift) trailing the babies Vincent and Ruth to see they did not fall into the lake. When Vincent and Ruth were a little older Hart had a grotto constructed for them, scooped out of an earthy bank and decorated with ferns. Water was diverted to form a small pool in which the children endlessly watched the antics of frogs and fish and turtles. To a small child it was a cavern out of fairyland filled by imagination with stalactites and stalagmites and other dripping mysteries.

A huge veranda surrounded Uncle Chester's cottage. Bessie remembers two lady campers standing on the smaller balcony beneath the eaves and singing operatic arias. "There was always someone singing or playing," she says. Younger Masseys have other memories. Ruth, aged seven or eight and captivated by a small Negro boy working around the camp in whose tent a dog named Socrates slept at night, rocked the family by sighing gustily, "Oh, I *wish* I was Soc!" Her younger sister Madeline, born in 1896, was baptized at the lake by Uncle Willard Perrin who with his wife, Susan's sister Nell, usually joined the summer camp. An Indian baby was baptized at the same time, and the romantic scene—the Indian couple paddling silently with their child across the sunlit, tree-girt lake for the ceremony—aroused a passionate envy in the heart of Dorothy, the third child of Walter and Susan, when she was old enough to recreate it in a highly imaginative mind.

In the big meeting-tent, furnished with sofas and turkey red cotton cushions and a harmonium, the family would gather, with the young men from Walter's Toronto Bible class and local residents by invitation, for conversation and talks and religious instruction, bawling Sankey and Moody hymns like "Throw Out The Life Line" with lusty enthusiasm. One of them, a youth named Charles Trick Currelly, had a passion for collecting things, and used to flit around the camp with a butterfly net. Like an arrow shot into the air, Walter's vivid stories of the Holy Land fell straight into the heart of young Currelly. Mesmerized by the beauty and mystery of the objects from ancient days he had seen in Walter's collection, he would devote his whole life with tireless patience to what was to become the Royal Ontario Museum, one of the finest in the world. Walter Massey's collection, eventually donated, was the nucleus of the Royal Ontario Museum.

Though the early 1890s were years of depression, the Massey-Harris organization continued to make progress. By 1893 total sales included more than half of all farm implements sold in Canada, amounting to $3,300,000.

For the great World's Columbian Exposition in Chicago in 1893, previews of the Massey-Harris display were held in Toronto, Brantford and Hamilton. The Toronto preview was held in the Massey Memorial Hall at the works and, the *Empire* reported, was attended by Mr. H. A. Massey and Miss Lilly Massey. A give-away booklet with a Union Jack cover was illustrated by the flags of all Massey-served countries, together with pertinent statistics for each one. The exhibit cost $10,000, and nine carloads of White-and-Gold implements went off to Chicago to win press acclaim across the continent. Many of the implements had moving parts that, lit by incandescent electric light, ran "smoothly as a watch" behind plate glass panels. Some of the conveyor belts were made of hand-embroidered silk. The company's office at the fair was constructed of all the highly

121

PICKERING TOWNSHIP PUBLIC LIBRARY
ROUGE HILL

polished native Canadian woods used in Massey-Harris implements. The firm's initials were formed by an arrangement of steel knives for reapers and mowers. Thoughtfully, a large number of comfortable chairs were provided at the exhibit. In company with a gigantic British flag hung more than sixty smaller flags from all the countries using Massey-Harris machinery. "Certainly," said the Chicago *Farm Implement News*, "it seems as if taste and workmanship could go no farther."

Press adulation, however, was not enough to win the awards the exhibit undoubtedly deserved, for a lamentable scandal developed in the judging, which resulted in a House of Commons request for investigation by the Canadian commissioner at the fair. It was at this exhibition that international juries had been replaced by single judges for each class—"results unsatisfactory," comments the *Encyclopaedia Britannica* laconically—and the company considered that it had been the victim of a deliberate swindle instigated by American competitors. Hart thundered accusations about award cards that had mysteriously disappeared from the exhibits, and even sections of the American press made shamefaced apology for the quality of the judging. Walter, who had accompanied the exhibit to Chicago, used some of his time at the fair to take a series of excellent photographs that were printed in *Massey's Illustrated*, reprinted in various newspapers, and won an accolade in the October issue of the *British Journal of Photography*.

Agricultural shows had been held annually in Ontario, rotated among the larger centres, from the time the first one was held in Toronto in 1846. For Toronto's second time around, in 1852, the *Canadian Journal* was able to record remarkable local development:

Not many years ago, the ground recently occupied by the provincial Agricultural Show, was a forest-covered tract and regarded by the citizens of York as altogether "in the country" and so inaccessible that when the late Hon. D'Arcy Boulton built the house in the field adjoining the clover pasture where the horses where [*sic*] exhibited, his *city* friends in amazement asked, "Who does he expect to visit him in that outlandish place." The most romantic believer in the future splendid destiny of Toronto, would have scarcely dared to suppose, that in one short generation, the forest wild would have become the judiciously chosen spot for a Canadian Provincial Show.

The grounds then covered about seventeen acres exclusive of the horse parade, nearly bisected by a winding but shallow ravine through which ran a pleasant stream. The exhibits were housed in five buildings and some large tents, with agricultural implements in the open. On Thursday, September twenty-third, the *Journal* reported proudly that no fewer than eleven hundred vehicles had passed through the toll-gate on Yonge Street near Yorkville, and about three hundred more had come in by the Davenport plank road.

The next provincial exhibition held in Toronto, in the year 1858, saw the erection of the Crystal Palace, an ambitious cruciform building of cast iron and glass two hundred and fifty-six feet long with an extreme width of a hundred and forty feet, a height from floor to ceiling of fifty-five feet, and four spacious stairs. For the patrons who flocked excitedly to see the new wonder of the modern age, there were trains leaving the foot of Simcoe Street every half hour for a fare of $12\frac{1}{2}$ cents, with weekly tickets at a dollar. The cab drivers had agreed to charge not more than 50 cents for the trip: parties of four would be charged 25¢ or 1/3d. each for a two-horse cab (one-horse cabs came a little cheaper at 1/- per person).

The Toronto Industrial Exhibition of 1879 opened in another and still more spacious location south of the old grounds and on the waterfront. Here it has remained, known today as the Canadian National Exhibition. Material from the Crystal Palace was used to construct the great exhibition building, the main feature of the sixty acres of grounds comprising the new site. It was on the old exhibition grounds, available when Hart and Charles Albert Massey came looking for a suitable place to locate their growing business, that the great Massey factory was built in the same year.

By 1886 Toronto's population was 110,000. "Ten years ago," wrote a gratified contemporary, "Toronto extended from the Don to Bathurst Street, from the Bay to College Street. Spadina Avenue north of St. Patrick was a field, and Sherbourne Street above Carlton Street was forest primeval." For one vision of the future this writer's crystal ball was clouded: "Spadina Avenue," he exclaimed, "this splendid avenue—the future 'Champs Elysees' of Toronto . . ."

Almost from the beginning of the Massey enterprise Hart had been a constant exhibitor at local, provincial and international fairs and field trials. As the Toronto Exhibition grew in importance, the Masseys competed with their own exhibit of the year before, each one offering a new attention-catching gimmick. Visitors crowded to hear the twenty-five-piece Massey Band, after a dashing entrance "in their new and superb wagon, drawn by four horses" and driven with a flourish by Hart himself. In 1886 crowds hung around the Massey stand to see "the first and only daily paper ever published at the Exhibition" produced before their very eyes. Their free copies of the chatty little *Bijou Bulletin*, illustrated with perky line drawings, gave them notice of exhibition events, weather conditions and topical news, with plenty of "plugs" for Massey products scattered throughout like raisins in a cake. "*Don't you forget* where I came from," the *Bulletin* warned its readers on the back page,"—red hot from the printing press driven by a Toronto Mower on end in the midst of the WHITE AND GOLD Harvesting Machines at the Toronto Industrial Exhibition, 1886—where you saw the mechanical figures representing the farmer and his wife exhibiting a Binder. . . . "

Grandstand shows of the day would be conversation topics for months. One attraction offered "the first magnificent display of fireworks and production of the most gorgeous spectacle ever exhibited in Canada, 'The Last Days of Pompeii' . . . Over 6,000 feet of painted scenery will be used in this grand spectacle, representing the City of Pompeii, Mount Vesuvius, and Bay of

124

Naples in the distance." In the more-colossal-than-ever tradition, the next year's show was "The Siege of Pekin [*sic*], a Pyrotechnic Spectacle introducing British, French and Chinese Troops, and British Seamen, presenting the most brilliant scene in this direction ever witnessed in Canada."

Special features, original and often amusing, continued to draw crowds to the Massey stand. A pair of mastiffs, Leo and Berno, applied dog-power to a binder one year. Life-size figures were grouped to form a vegetable wedding:

The blushing Bride is in the form of a young Tomato [foreshadowing the slang of a later age?] while the nervous Groom is green Cucumber. A ponderous Cabbage bears the likeness of the pompous and self-important Magistrate and the solemn Notary is found in the Horse Radish. The face of the Mother-in-law appears in the leafy folds of an ample Cauliflower, Guests are there in the forms of Celery and Carrot, Musicians are represented by Beans and Peas, Witnesses by Asparagus and Onion, and the smart little Page by the Radish.

For the 1890 Exhibition, a fifteen-foot working model of one of the Massey Toronto freight trains was driven by electricity around a circular track. But the real feature of the company's exhibit that year was the romantic figure of Halil Yousef, the Egyptian dragoman, who came back into the lives of the Masseys in a ludicrous incident seized upon by the anti-Massey *Evening News* in a tear-jerking story of injustice.

With a picture of the gentleman in baggy-trousered native dress, the story of his arrival in Toronto had been announced in *Massey's Illustrated* for August, 1890.

Who is Halil Yousef? He is a native of Cairo, Egypt—an Egyptian Arab of the better class, and who at home is known as a dragoman or guide and interpreter. He speaks four different languages—Arabic, English, French, and Italian, and can make himself understood in German. He is making a brief sojourn in Canada, and it has been arranged for him to be present at the Industrial Exhibition, Toronto, where he will appear in native costume, never having worn any other. . . .
Yousef (Joseph) travelled through the Orient with Messrs. W. E. H. Massey and his brother, the late Fred. V. Massey, for a

period of about two months, acting as guide and interpreter, etc. The Orientals are a very friendly and kind-hearted people. He became much attached to the Messrs. Massey, and especially to Mr. Fred, with whom he formed a very warm friendship, which was strongly evinced in their parting, when Joseph wept like a child. As a mark of his esteem, he took from his finger a handsomely wrought gold ring, in which was mounted a valuable ancient scarabœus, and presented it to Mr. Fred. Halil Yousef is the possessor of some considerable property in Cairo, and determined as soon as he could realize on it, to visit his new-found Canadian friends, and further, having been with Mr. Massey when he sold the first reaping machine at Jerusalem, Palestine, he became interested in hearing of the great Canadian harvesting machine works.

During Mr. Fred Massey's long illness, a letter from Halil announced his intention of coming to Canada next year. Word was sent back, however, by Mr. Fred, that he could not hope to live but a few months, and, if he would see him again on earth, to come at once. Pained to hear of his illness, and most anxious to see him again, Joseph started. He had, however, only gotten as far as London, Eng., on his way, when he learned . . . of Mr. Fred's death. His great grief at this news was sad to see. At first he was for turning back, but after consideration decided to come on and visit his dear friend's grave—a thing that is always considered a highly esteemed privilege by the Orientals—and to become acquainted with the other members of the family, and see the great reaper works. Hence he came.

Since arrival, he has been busying himself at the office of the Massey Manufacturing Co. He will remain during the Industrial Exhibition, and will daily exhibit the Toronto light binder on the stand of the Massey Manufacturing Co., where the company's patrons may make his acquaintance. At the close of the Exhibition Halil returns home, with a firm determination to do his part to further the interests of Massey-Toronto machines in the Orient, where they have already been introduced. Halil is confident that it is only a question of time when self-binders will supplant the cheap labor and old time reaping hooks still in general use in his native land.

The Oriental gentleman, however, considered his welcome to Toronto to have been very different from what he had expected, and thought he had been grossly ill-used by the Masseys. His complaints were so loud and so long that the *News* blew him up into a front-page story, announced that he was about to sue

Mr. Massey, and printed "his unvarnished story guilelessly told in broken English with tears starting from his eyes."

"I am a dragoman or Oriental guide with headquarters at Cairo. I show the pyramids and other historical places in the East to travellers, and contract to take them through the Holy Land and show the holy places when they wish to take in that extended trip. I provide camels, provisions and everything complete. A couple of years ago in Cairo I met Mr. Walter E. H. Massey and the late Mr. Fred V. Massey, and contracted to show them through Egypt and the Holy Land. They were then on their great tour of the world, which was known to Toronto people. We made the trip going as far as Jerusalem, and formed a strong friendship and said farewell when we returned to Egypt. Walter Massey said when parting that I might do well in Canada with my money if I was to sell out and go there; also that they would be pleased to entertain me if I ever came.

"The matter of my going to America stopped at that point until Mr. Fred Massey was taken ill. He then commenced writing letters to me saying that he would like to see me before he died. I could not read English writing but got the letters translated at Cairo. They became more importunate until I received nearly a dozen and W. E. H. Massey also wrote indorsing [*sic*] his brother's request. I was finally asked 'to come for God's sake' and see the dying young man, and I started. The inducement of being employed by the firm was held out. I was directed to go to the London, England, office of the firm and pay my fare that far, and my expenses would there be refunded and the London agent would give me money to come on to Toronto. I arrived in London and . . . learned that Mr. H. A. Massey was on his way to London and that Fred had just died. I was sent to a hotel to await Mr. Massey's arrival in London.

"When Mr. Massey arrived he said, Well, what will you do now? Will you return? saying at the same time that Miss Massey, his daughter, was very anxious that I should come on to Toronto and be present at the next Toronto Industrial Exhibition to aid in advertising the exhibit of the Massey Company.

"I did not like to return to Cairo immediately, as I left there with the hope of making money and my sudden return would have occasioned ridicule. Finally I agreed to come on to Toronto. Mr. Massey said he would pay my way here and back to Cairo. I was to stay three months as his guest and if I stayed any longer I was to assist at the Exhibition. I was to receive $20 per month, though I have often made that amount in a day.

"I reached Toronto one Sunday night four months ago, and was taken to the Massey residence, Jarvis Street. Instead of being treated according to my rank and expectation, for I had servants of my own, I was put to work the morning after my arrival to sweep the sidewalk in front of the residence, split wood, pull little weeds out of the lawn grass and all kinds of menial work. When a new gardener and coachman arrived, I was sent to help him to move his furniture to the coachman's residence. This went on until two days ago, when heartsick and weary I left the Massey residence, having stayed six weeks over my three months and receiving no pay at all.

"Mr. Massey now contends that I was working for my board, and that he did not promise to send me back to Egypt, and that I came to this country on my own responsibility. He says his son was under the influence of morphine when he wrote these letters. I walked down Jarvis to King Street when I left the house and was followed by a great crowd attracted by my costume. Standing on King Street and not knowing where to go I was hailed by a gentleman passing in a carriage, who addressed me in Arabic. It was Dr. James Ward-el-Ward, whom I had known ten years ago in Jerusalem, who was speaking. I immediately recognized him when he spoke. His family is one of the most aristocratic and ancient of Jerusalem. They have been there continuously since several centuries before the Jewish captivity.

"Mr. [sic] Ward-el-Ward brought me home with him, where I have been since. We have seen Mr. Massey and my case is being pushed. I am very anxious to get home before the cold weather sets in. Mr. Massey at first refused to do anything, but reconsidered that decision, and promised to see Mr. Ward-el-Ward to-night. Legal opinion holds that he is liable. I have pawned all my jewelry and valuables since I came and gave $150 in presents of Eastern laces and shawls to members of the Massey family. My gold watch was stolen in Italy while coming here. If everything else fails I will get up a lecture on Egypt and tell my story in Shaftesbury hall. I am sure the Christian people of Toronto in that event would support me, as I must go home."

Yousef weeps bitterly over his disappointment and misfortunes. Yesterday he visited the College Street fire hall and cried as if his heart would break. He fears he will freeze to death if winter arrives before he escapes to hot Egyptian climes, which he has always been accustomed to.

Five days later the impulsive dragoman was busy retracting much of his story, and the *News* had lost some of its initial

128

enthusiasm for its protégé. For the next instalment, the tone of the reporting had become lightly jocular:

Yousef, the gentleman with the baggy pantaloons and the fez, who hails from Bagdad or Cairo or somewhere, the yellow man whom the Masseys brought out here in the fulness of their hearts as an advertisement of their enterprise, treated THE NEWS staff to an Oriental scene this morning by casting himself on the floor and wailing as they do in the East. It is clear that Yousef wants to crawl out of his original statements regarding his treatment, and with that view he brought a letter to this office from Wad-el-Ward [sic]. Whether Wad-el-Ward is an Indian fakeer or an Egyptian mystic we do not know, nor can we find how he came to blow into this controversy, but Yousef came in with his letter, so there must be some friendship between them. The soft-mannered young man who presides in the reporters' room thought the letter an impertinence, and he refused to publish it, whereupon Yousef pointed a long lean yellow finger at the ceiling and besought Allah to help him, and then he sat down in the doorway near a stove kept in the hall for winter use, and groaned and sputtered and . . . reached for the stove as if to get some ashes to cast upon his head. Rather than call up the wagon it was agreed that the letter be published, and here it is:

"EDITOR NEWS: The history of my troubles, which you print in your paper of last evening, and which has been carefully read to me, is in many respects wholly incorrect. Your paper states that I said certain things which I did not say, and which are not true. I therefore must ask space to correct these errors, as it injures my cause and puts me in a false position.

"In the first place, I never intimated to your reporter that I thought of going to law over our differences. Mr. Massey, when he met me in London, asked me what I wished to do. I told him, 'As Mr. Fred is dead, I do not think it best for me to go on to Canada.' Mr. Massey at first thought so too, and even went so far as to secure my passage back to my home, but after this he asked me to go to my lodgings and reconsider whether I would go on or back. The agreement was that I was to remain with Mr. Massey as butler and do light service, and not as 'guest,' as your paper states, for three months, in consideration of which he was to pay my fare from London to Toronto and back, and moreover I agreed that if I stayed over the three months I was to get $20 per month. I have only been here a little over two months and certainly did not tell your reporter I have worked six weeks over three months without receiving pay. Mr. Massey and his family treated me well; as I told them, except that the

129

service was distasteful to me and not what I agreed it would be, hence I left his house.

"My principal difference with Mr. Massey was regarding my return fare at the end of the first three months. I claim that he agreed to pay my return fare, which he says he did not. Mr. Massey offered some weeks ago to loan me the money for my return at the end of the first three months, but as I did not feel it right, especially after our London agreement, I being homesick, without friends, and so far away from home, was only too glad to accept a loan rather than bring more trouble, but when I found that I was made to do menial work, and not because of the exhibition, I left his house.

"I did not bring any Eastern laces with me, hence I could not have stated that I gave $150 worth of these goods to the Massey family, though I did give them a few things.

"I deeply regret that my story was exaggerated in your paper and most humbly pray you to publish these corrections. Yours, etc., Jas. Wad-el-Ward, For Joseph Khalul [sic], His X sign, Toronto, Aug. 23rd, 1890."

Though the *News* had now reduced Yousef to a comic-strip character, it could not overlook the opportunity of another tart dig at the Masseys: "They brought him here and should be responsible for his return. There are plenty of men in this country wanting such work as Yousef was put to and there is no occasion to import them, no matter how picturesque they may look."

The interest of the *Evening News* petered out with its final report on September first:

Poor Halil Yousef, the Mahommedan dragoman, has not yet left for his loved though distant Cairo. From present appearances he will stay for the great Toronto Exhibition, though he is fairly shivering these days when he goes outside, notwithstanding the fact that he has added a capacious overcoat to his Oriental habit. He thinks this is a dreadfully cold climate, and calls on Allah to protect him when accosted about his return.

He is staying now at H. A. Massey's office and sleeps in the building somewhere, taking his meals with the janitor. It is probable that Mr. Massey has induced the stranger to stay for the Exhibition to fulfil the announcement made in *Massey's Illustrated* that Yousef would be at the Exhibition with a Massey reaper.

Some other firm which makes reapers announced that it would have an Arab figure at the Exhibition, fixed up in Eastern costume, and the Massey company apparently want to get ahead by having a real live Oriental. Meanwhile Yousef sighs for the parching land of the pyramids and the Pharaohs.

The rest, as far as the *News* was concerned, was silence. The *Mail*, however, picked up the conclusion of the story in its September thirteen edition. "The Egyptian Dragoman, Halil Yousef, is an object of much interest to the crowds which surround the mammoth exhibit of the Massey Manufacturing Company, in the Agricultural hall. Halil Yousef is daily to be seen there, dressed in his attractive Oriental costume. The exhibit of Massey & Co. this year is finer than ever, if such a thing is possible."

After which, Halil Yousef bade good-bye to Canada and thankfully departed for a warmer clime.

Good Works

Not quite a year after Hart Massey's death, his much-loved only daughter Lillian married at the age of almost forty-three. Perhaps it was her own shyness that had postponed marriage until now; perhaps recurring illness had seemed to make marriage inadvisable; perhaps Hart's possessive devotion had driven off interested suitors. On at least one occasion Susan remembered her father-in-law awaiting Lillian's return from a concert with her escort, standing in the front hall and shredding the leaves of a potted plant in his agitation. Hart had found in his gentle wife a woman of her generation whose whole life was bound up in her home and children. His daughter, with a surprising understanding of business detail for one so sheltered, could listen while he talked about company matters and often make suggestions her father was glad to adopt. He took Lillian to Europe with him on many occasions and left her, when he died, an equal executor of his estate with her two brothers.

A hint has come down of a deeply emotional association between Lillian and an unnamed man. Does a mysterious document, filed with but rejected as part of her will and sealed by a Surrogate Court judge, hold a part of this secret?

The man who eventually became Lillian Massey's husband was John Mill Treble, a haberdasher with grown children whose "Great Shirt House" had been established in 1865 at the corner of King and Bay streets in premises "handsome, commodious and elegantly equipped." His first wife had died in 1887. John Treble was a shrewd businessman who had early realized the value of advertising. In nearly every descriptive book on Toronto published through the years, the reader was enjoined to visit "one of the handsomest retail stores in the city."

A stout pompous man with a benevolent but humourless expression, John Treble was a native Torontonian "highly esteemed in both social and commercial circles for his many excellent qualities and integrity." His sole interest, apart from his "Perfect Fitting French Yoke Shirts" manufactured up on the third floor by "fifteen to twenty-five hands," was in the advancement of Methodist church activities. He had lived for several years in a small house on Breadalbane Street, and moved in 1885 to a thin three-storey red brick house with an unusually tall, narrow gable, at 387 (now 443) Jarvis Street, not far from the Massey home. His attentions to Lillian had been persistent, and for a long time they were received with lukewarm interest: only days before she announced her acceptance of his suit, Lillian's response to the information that Mr. Treble awaited her in the drawing-room was so unenthusiastic that fifteen-year-old Bessie, on a visit to the family home and sent downstairs to entertain her aunt's elderly suitor, was convinced he was about to receive a final dismissal.

The couple left for a two-month honeymoon in Europe after the ceremony in the drawing-room of Euclid Hall at one o'clock on January twenty-sixth, 1897, where Lillian was attended by her cousin, Ida Boate (daughter of Hart's sister Frances), with Master Vincent Massey as page and seven-year-old Ruth as maid of honour. The bridegroom's gift to the bride was a Bible. Lillian would not be denied her white wedding. Her dress of heavy white satin trimmed with orange blossom had leg-of-mutton sleeves, a boned bodice, and a skirt with a long train, richly lined with lace and so finely gored that it could not be used afterwards for anything but a doll's wedding dress, made years later by Walter's youngest daughter for a daughter of her own. Lillian's exquisite veil of rose point Brussels lace was matched by a fan from Paris, which she carried at the small reception that followed. "Be careful of the veil, Lilly," warned her mother.

"Ruth is to have that." It has since been worn by Ruth herself and many other Massey brides.

Lillian was often ill, though no doctor was able to diagnose what troubled her. On one of the occasions when her indisposition held up the little party that travelled to San Francisco in 1887 to see "the boys" off to Australia, Lillian had been highly indignant when the doctor flatly informed her there was nothing wrong. Though she spent much time confined to bed or resting on a chaise-longue in the sun porch upstairs, she still managed to execute with surprisingly persistent shrewdness an impressive number of projects. She completely made over the family home, installing an elevator and an electric organ, moving the main stairway to a different location, adding bathrooms and redecorating the main rooms, including an oriental room bordered with scalloped arches and slim pillars whose capitals were coloured in blue, red, green and gold. (It is probable that the decorative style of Massey Hall owes much to Lillian's influence, accustomed as her father was to turn to her for discussion of his projects.) Oriental rugs covered the parquet floor and luxury was implicit in dark blue plush couches with heavy mahogany frames, small carved taboret tables and elegant, but uncomfortable, chairs of curved wood inlaid with mother-of-pearl. The redecorated house spelled glamour and romance to Massey children and Massey guests, who fondly recall their delight in Lillian's Moorish room.

Quick to observe ideas in the area of her interest, she was also quick to translate them into action. Assistance given inexperienced travellers in New York inspired her to initiate, through the Woman's Christian Temperance Union, the Toronto branch of the Travellers' Aid Society in 1903.

The most enduring monument she left is the solid School of Household Science building at the corner of Bloor Street and Avenue Road in midtown Toronto, which she had erected, equipped and presented to the University of Toronto. Lillian's dreams and ideals took intensely practical form. When her father presented the building for the Fred Victor Mission, it was Lillian

134

who took over the details. "Largely at her suggestion and under her leadership," said Dr. R. P. Bowles, Chancellor of Victoria University, "changes were made and the Mission grew into a highly organized institution with many different activities."

Lillian's chief interest had been in the work with women and girls at the mission. There, sixty to seventy small girls would gather in the "Kitchen Garden" classes. With child-size tables, dainty white cloths, tiny sets of dishes and cutlery, little brooms tied with ribbons and diminutive washday sets, they learned to enjoy the necessities of housekeeping. In cooking classes, as they grew older, they worked at long tables with individual sets of cooking utensils, wearing long, all-enveloping white aprons.

As she became impressed by the value of proper training, Lillian devoted the top floor of the building, and then an additional building, to what became the Lillian Massey School of Household Science. Under the authority and with the sanction and assistance of the Department of Education of Ontario, the school could offer "a thorough course of Normal instruction for teachers of Household Science" covering (in junior year) chemistry, physics, biology, psychology and pedagogy, history or education, household economics, hygiene, applied cookery and laundry, observation of teaching of public school children, and adding (in senior year) food analysis, physiology, bacteriology, domestic architecture, home nursing and emergencies, practice teaching, planning courses for children, dietetics, marketing and household accounts. Student teachers instructed the children who had graduated from the "Kitchen Garden" classes. There was even a very common-sense *LMS Book of Recipes*.

When the University of Toronto became interested in establishing a degree course in household science, Lillian offered to provide a building. The first sod was turned in July, 1908, and the building was formally opened in January, 1913, though it had been in use before completion: the students went up fire-escape

135

Kinsale Association Library

ladders to work on the top floors before the bottom ones were ready.

A solid square Greek-style building with walls almost two feet thick, it looks today like a relic of another age but remains unexpectedly functional. Lillian had travelled throughout the United States to study the latest building developments. From her bedroom, she directed every detail of construction, pored over every cost sheet, every blueprint.

"Is that the best material available?" she would ask.

"No, but it's perfectly adequate."

"Use the better material," Lillian would order. Entrance hall and main stairway were built entirely of white Italian marble, the upper landing supported by marble Ionic columns. Woodwork throughout was solid oak, even the lockers (for five hundred students) in the basement, where a forty-five-by-twenty-foot white-tiled swimming pool and a two-storey-high gymnasium provided athletic facilities. A second row of radiators was installed in the gymnasium below the upper windows in readiness for the day when the addition of a floor would create another needed room. Adjoining the dressing-rooms was a hair-drying room designed by Lillian herself, with outlets from a hot-air pipe. Lavish equipment in all departments (Limoges china, acid-resistant stone or solid marble table-tops for laboratory work) was augmented by several of Lillian's own ingenious ideas. Tables for dressmaking classes were of varnished softwood that would take pins, for instance, and blackboards were of ground glass backed by green paper, whose threaded string grid providing guidelines behind the glass has never had to be replaced in fifty years of use. Every drawer in the built-in oak cupboards fitted smoothly, and had its own lock. The visual-aid lantern for the one hundred-and-twenty-five-seat auditorium was in use until 1953. Only equipment outdated by technical advances has needed replacement. "It's a woman's building," says the present dean, Dr. Barbara McLaren, "planned carefully to meet the needs of women."

136

To the building she presented to Mount Allison Ladies' College at Sackville, New Brunswick, and which became the nucleus of the Home Economics Department of Mount Allison University, Lillian gave the same careful attention and studied the plans just as exhaustively, even to the description of the woodbox.

After his marriage to Lillian, John Treble gave up much of his business activity to attend to the financial affairs of the Fred Victor Mission and the Deaconess Home (now demolished) on St. Clair Avenue and Avenue Road, a building to which Lillian had given financial support and critical attention. She had even managed to attend the sod-turning ceremony on May first, 1908, though she watched it from the seat of her victoria.

Then on May seventeenth, 1909, about to take his seat at the great round mahogany boardroom table in the Massey-Harris offices as a recently elected director, John Treble had a heart seizure and died instantly at the age of sixty-three, in the twelfth year of his marriage to Lillian.

Lillian herself lived until 1915. After many years of worsening health, she died at the age of sixty-two in Santa Barbara, "one of California's numerous health resorts," Walter had written when the travellers stayed there for a few days in 1887, "so situated on the bend of the coast as to be defended from the cold coast winds, [with] a remarkably warm, equable climate." She left an estate of more than two million dollars and among her assets was listed a small island, Cedar Island on Lake Rosseau, which she had bought because it was in the pollen-free area but which she used very little. Four-tenths of an acre in size, it was reached by a little steam yacht and almost covered by the building she erected on it.

One of her greatest delights in latter years had been listening to Toronto's Metropolitan Church organ over a special telephone receiver set she had had installed on a private line from the church; and among numerous charitable bequests she left a

$61,000 endowment fund for the organ, which with complicated terms included the salary of a specifically qualified organist and twenty free annual public recitals. If her detailed conditions could not be fulfilled, the income was to go to the benefit of sick, disabled or aged professional organists who had served in any evangelical church in Toronto for five years or more.

As a memorial to her husband, fifty thousand dollars was to be invested to pay the salaries of teachers to instruct poor women and children in household arts at the Fred Victor Mission. After her relatives and friends had been cared for, the Department of Household Science at the University of Toronto, Victoria University and various departments of the Methodist church also received large bequests.

In 1897 Walter Massey, who had been president of the company since his father's death a year earlier, had begun an exciting new venture: a two-hundred-and-forty-acre farm, which he named Dentonia Park, for his wife Susan Denton, "beautifully situated on the highlands just north-east of Toronto, one of the healthiest spots in Ontario." Now a part of Metro Toronto, and bounded roughly by Danforth Avenue, Dawes Road, Medhurst Road and Pharmacy Avenue, the rolling, wooded area had been a series of market gardens, discarded villa lots and waste lands. More than thirty deeds were needed to consolidate these into one property.

Under Walter's management, it was turned into a model farm and country estate, where he and his elder brother Chester built big summer homes, and where Walter carried on advanced agricultural experiments and eventually a scheme (through the agency of the City Dairy Company, which he founded) to provide a safe milk supply for Toronto.

From the time he had been brought home from Boston to play a full-time role in the firm, Walter's life had been crammed full of activity. To the main business of the company—the production of agricultural implements—had been added, in

1895, a separate five-storey factory for the manufacture of "wheels," expected to turn out about five to ten thousand vehicles a year. "The bicycle," Walter announced, "is not simply a fad, but it has become a thoroughly practical vehicle for use on the farm as well as in the city and in the village." By September, 1896, $16,000-worth of them had been shipped to Australia, and in 1897 *The New Zealand Cyclist* reported that the winner of the five-mile Victorian championship at Melbourne had ridden a Massey-Harris racer. As well, the Massey-Toronto Carriage and Implement Emporium at 126 King Street East was offering all kinds of vehicles, including surreys, buggies, mikados, spider phaetons, sulkies and democrat wagons. At Dentonia Park, the busy industrialist became a "gentleman farmer" with the wholehearted involvement he brought to everything he undertook.

Forty acres of the "plain and woodland, lake, stream, hill and dale" of his estate were kept as parkland. Most of the rest of it had specific purposes to serve. He had imported herds of Jersey thoroughbreds, of Ayrshires and Shropshire cattle, and a four-storey barn built into a steep hillside with facilities for driving in on every level was a model of ingenuity, many of its innovations being his own idea and design. Revolving funnels on the ridge of the roof carried fresh air to the ground floor where the cattle being fattened and the small herds of picked Berkshire and Yorkshire swine in especially constructed pens were located. The second floor held the Jerseys and, through a heavy fireproof door, the dynamo and working dairy. The horses and carriages, the workshops and the rooms for grooms, herdsmen and other employees were on the third floor. The top floor was the barn proper, a storage for feed and straw conveyed by chutes to where it was needed.

All the attendants were required to wear white coats, and music was piped in to soothe the cows as they were milked. A completely sanitary laboratory, where milk was "modified" according to a process used in the Walker-Gordon Laboratories of Boston to make it easier for infants to digest, had fully tiled walls, an asphalt floor, glass tables and shelves and a solid porcelain sink.

Dentonia's 170-by-16-foot poultry house, whose third floor held grinders, clover- and meat-cutters run by windmill power, was divided into sixteen pens, with a forty-eight-foot run for each pen, to accommodate five hundred laying hens. Fresh eggs as well as table fowls were delivered to city customers, as was milk from the dairy, the modified milk being supplied only on physicians' prescriptions. Dentonia also had a well-developed fisheries department, which supplied market trout in season, and eggs, fry and trout for stocking streams and ponds throughout the province.

A visit to Dentonia became a local Toronto event—visitors were welcome any day except Sunday—either by individuals or in groups who were met at the terminus of the street railway "by tally-hos drawn by four spirited horses."

His influential position in the community brought Walter into demand as a public speaker, and to this chore he brought not only hard-driving facts but a sense of humour that must have enlivened many a dull meeting. At the annual dinner of the Canadian Manufacturers' Association in August, 1900, for instance, he began by a serious examination of the need to better Canada's position in export trade. He deplored the lack of good export facilities in Montreal and Quebec, pointing out that out of some fifteen hundred carloads shipped to the Atlantic seaboard by his company in the previous season, not one had gone through a Canadian port. He reminded his audience that Canada was now a manufacturing country whose exports were no longer only lumber and cheese, and no detail should be too small for an exporter's attention. Awareness that machines despatched unvarnished would save customs duties in some countries and care in packing, so that a machine did not arrive with two of one part and none of another, had not only added to profits in his own firm but had created goodwill among its customers.

Then, when his listeners were settling their faces into masks of studious attention to a further series of statistics and injunctions, he concluded solemnly:

Attention paid to the advertising habits of other countries will avoid the predicament of one of our competitors who sent to Germany a quantity of posters that would have drawn gratifying results in North America. The illustration showed a mowing machine driven by the Goddess of Liberty in full color, in shining and polychromatic garments of scanty proportions, and drawn by a team of Bengal tigers. In due course he received an agitated letter from his bewildered German agent. "The picture of your admirable machine," the agent wrote with desperate politeness, "of which I the receipt of ten thousand acknowledge, is not useful in this country, and it is of much regret to me that I request to return them permission. The women of our country, when by circumstances to do agricultural work compelled, do not dress, as your picture shows, is the custom in your wonderful country, and would not even deem such garments with modesty to consist. Also, we do not tigers for draught purposes cultivate, they not being to the country native, nor in our experience, for such work well suited. I have to my customers explained with earnestness that your picture is an allegory, and does not mean that your admirable machine should be operated by women too little clothed, nor is it necessary that the place of horses shall be animals from the Zoologischer Garten be taken. I cannot use them as you instruct."

In 1901 all Toronto was agog with the excitement of a royal visit. Local papers had followed with palpitating journalese the cross-country travels of Their Royal Highnesses the Duke and Duchess of York, "the future King and Queen of the British Empire," from their first landing on Canadian soil after the royal yacht *Ophir* anchored off Quebec City on September fifteenth, and throughout the trip by royal train to British Columbia and back. Torontonians read about the greeting of Indians in full costume in Calgary, the fleet of canoes that

141

paddled over five miles of Lake Manitoba to take His Royal Highness to a shooting lodge, the great arch of wheat sheaves beneath which the royal carriage had passed in Winnipeg, the bonfires lighted at Rat Portage. Only a few days before the arrival of the Duke and Duchess, the world had been shocked by the assassination of United States President McKinley; Canadians were glad to find something happier to read about in their newspapers.

Toronto got ready with uninhibited enthusiasm. The streets were hung with banners, buildings were draped with bunting, and enormous arches were erected by various civic and commercial bodies at strategic spots on the route of the royal procession. By general agreement, the most significant of these was the Independent Order of Foresters' arch at Bay and Richmond streets, a four-fronted arch supporting a dome surmounted by a Tudor crown, the globe on top of the crown sporting a Maltese cross, the whole outlined in red, white and blue lights, with about a hundred Royal Foresters stationed over the four curves of the arch and trumpeters grouped at the corners to sound a fanfare upon Their Highnesses' arrival.

Newspaper readers were entertained by vivid descriptions with drawings of the lavishly furnished royal apartments at Government House, effectively contradicting the legend that still persists—and will continue to persist, since people love a legend—that the Duke and Duchess stayed at the Massey home on Jarvis Street. There was another reason why the royal couple would have been unlikely guests at the home of the Methodist haberdasher and his wealthy, ailing wife. Lillian's younger brother Walter had not been well since his return from an important business trip to Ottawa at the end of September, and by the time of the royal visit his deteriorating condition was causing acute anxiety in the whole family.

The general public, eagerly scanning every snippet of intimate detail, learned that the Duke's room, in reversal of the traditional colours for male and female, was decorated in pink and white, the Duchess's in blue and white. The Duke's bedstead in the

142

colonial style of black mahogany, with four massive carved corner posts and the royal arms carved in relief on the low headboard, was said to be one used by George III. The morning room, following the antique style of decor "everywhere evident and yet not overdone," was hung below a frieze of ferociously floral wallpaper with pictures of Their Highnesses' royal relatives, among them George III and Queen Charlotte, George IV, William IV and the late Queen with Prince Arthur.

The Parliament Buildings had been outlined with electric lights, the trees in Queen's Park hung with Chinese lanterns. In lyrical cliché, the whole city was "a veritable fairy-land." In an optimistic experiment, "a new design for a Canadian flag ... formed part of the decorations on the branch of the Canadian Bank of Commerce at the corner of College and Yonge streets ... [the] design has the usual Union Jack in the corner, while on the red ground are placed seven maple leaves in blue, emblematic of the seven Provinces, which would be increased as additions were made to Confederation."

The royal moment was at hand. "The heir-apparent," announced the *Daily Mail and Empire* on October tenth, "has been advancing toward Toronto all day through the rocky wilderness of New Ontario, which he crossed this way to the West a fortnight ago." Thousands had flocked to the city, especially to the environs of the magnificent new City Hall, which had been opened on September eighteenth, 1899, just over two years earlier, at a cost of two and a half million dollars. The official procedures had been organized for minute-by-minute execution, and there had been the usual jealous jockeying for position, with Alderman Lynd asking if members of city council would be presented individually and Alderman Sheppard gloomily supposing that common aldermen would have to "tag after some other persons." "Every element of success is assured," said the *Mail and Empire* "excepting good weather."

The weather, alas, did not co-operate. The five-column drawing of the presentation of addresses at the City Hall in next day's paper showed a dismal sea of umbrellas and the rain slanting down over wet and shining streets. "Oh," sighed the *Mail and Empire*, "for a glint of sunshine to have lighted up the pageant!"

But it could console itself—and did—with the enthusiasm of the city's welcome:

To Toronto belongs the glory of the very climax of Canada's welcome to the heir-apparent. And why not to Toronto—loyal Toronto—the heart of English-speaking Canada, the great centre of Imperial impulse, and first among cities of Greater Britain in devotion to the British flag and the British Crown, a devotion more than once sealed with her blood?

That Toronto's welcome especially impressed the Royal pair as one of the most enthusiastic in their triumphal tour around the greater part of the world was made known by exclamations which fell from their own lips.

"Splendid, splendid," said the Duke, as cheer after cheer went up from the rain-soaked multitude.

"It is exquisite, simply exquisite," the Duchess was heard to remark during one of the selections of the Royal chorus.

At one moment in the ceremony it must have been difficult for the royal pair to maintain their studied calm. Mixed signals brought Mr. Torrington's fifteen-hundred-voice Royal Chorus to its feet in a burst of glorious song just as the mayor began to read the civic address of welcome. Frantic gestures proved of no avail; Mr. Torrington was wholeheartedly engrossed in his music, and "fifteen hundred Canadians were singing about their Country and their King." An alderman had to be despatched to tug at the conductor's sleeve before the song petered out into embarrassed silence and the address could continue.

The City Hall ceremony gave the *Globe* an opportunity for prophetic utterance. "The children who sang 'The Maple Leaf Forever' yesterday," it predicted, "will live to see that simple leaf the emblem of a great people."

Instead of a dramatic performance, since the Court was still in official mourning for Queen Victoria, a concert in Massey Music Hall was the featured entertainment for the evening of the

144

great day, the opening of a three-day music festival. Souvenir programmes on white satin were delicately embellished with coats of arms, entwined initials and St. George spearing the dragon. The centre of the balcony was equipped as a royal loge, and "even from the festoons of greenery," said the *Globe* "peeped shy lights of various hues." With Canadian maple leaves, red and white roses, thousands of yards of "the laurels of merry England" (specially imported) and white lace over a turkey red background, it was a resplendent scene.

The royal party was late in arriving, and the guest singer, Madame Calvé, who had delayed her opening song as long as she could, was caught in the middle of it when "God Save The King" drowned her out and the audience turned its back on her to stare at the Duke and Duchess. "Probably no singer ever fought against greater odds than Madame Calvé," commented the *Mail and Empire* next day. "In her several numbers she had to sing first against a brass band out on the street, then against a chorus of fish-horns, then against a cavalcade of fire-engines and hose reels, and finally against a band of pipers. When the pibroch sounded it was too much for the risibilities of her listeners."

None of the Masseys was in attendance at the Music Hall that evening, and the royal pair expressed their regret when apologies were presented on behalf of Mr. W. E. H. Massey and Mr. C. D. Massey. Out at Dentonia Walter was struggling with the dread disease that had carried off his eldest brother.

It was the most tragic of ironies that Walter Massey, a man in the very forefront of active example and pressure for greater attention to sanitation and hygiene, should become a victim of typhoid fever. At the peak of a brilliant career, he was only thirty-seven when his death came with stunning suddenness on October twenty-eighth, 1901, and left a gap in many circles. The sense of loss in all of them was genuine, for Walter Massey was one of those rare people whose abilities were matched by a

145

kind heart and a personality of real charm. Workmen who could nurse a strong personal resentment against his father were inclined to separate Walter in their minds from responsibility for what they regarded as the shortcomings of the company. He had been president of Massey-Harris since Hart's death, as well as a director and president of numerous other companies. He had been a regent of Victoria University and held other executive positions in the Methodist Church.

The boys who had been members of the Young Men's Bible League that he had founded in 1891 at the Central Methodist Church, Bloor Street, were especially bereaved. Walter always prepared for the classes with infinite care, studying the day's subject and making copious notes for reference. "He had a way of bringing a story vividly alive," said a contemporary. Here his personal knowledge of the Holy Land was a great advantage, and he used it with inspiring effect. In the big house at 550 Jarvis Street that he had bought in 1898 he had furnished a downstairs room for "my boys" of the Bible League, where he entertained them every Tuesday evening. In summer, his Bible class at Dentonia Park Farm was attended by more than seventy employees and friends every Sunday.

One friend who would miss Walter had grown up in Newcastle as an underprivileged small boy whose widowed mother made a living by boarding Massey workmen, and whose first job, at fourteen, was in the local woollen mill, of which Hart Massey was president. This was the young Joseph Atkinson who, taught to blame the "bosses" for everything from low wages to his mother's early death through hard work and worry, and who had resented the affluence of nine-years-older Walter, later took a failing evening paper and built it into today's powerful *Toronto Star*. Walter Massey was one of three Toronto men who put $10,000 into the venture, and Atkinson came to value his elder-statesman advice and support.

But his loss was felt most keenly by his family and close friends. Now Susan must go upstairs alone to look on her sleeping children—"One of my luxuries," Walter used to say fondly as he stood by Susan's side in the darkened room each evening. But Susan had the strength to pick up the threads of her broken life with courage and capability, building the life for their children that her husband would have wanted. Her sister Nell and brother-in-law the Reverend Willard Perrin, who had been constant and welcome visitors through the years, eventually came to live at Dentonia on retirement, and for years energetic cheerful Uncle Willard, a Harvard Phi Beta Kappa and nationally famous athlete, "stood in" as father for the young Masseys. In the best Massey organ-giving tradition, Susan presented an organ to the Central Methodist Church in Walter's memory. Hart had given one to the Methodist Assembly at Chautauqua in the early days, and Lillian had one installed in the Metropolitan Church on Queen Street.

Walter had found his wife's astute judgment helpful in business matters: now she took over the administration of the estate, taking an active part in Massey-Harris affairs, maintaining the town house and overseeing the organization of the farm and its various departments. It was no small undertaking for a woman of those days. She planned and remodelled farm buildings as needed, sub-contracting the work of building cottages for the permanent staff and a boarding hall for farm workers. With a hundred and thirty acres of arable land devoted to agriculture, fifty acres of well-shaded and well-watered pasture land, the feed barn, the cow barn, the four-storey main barn, ten acres of market gardens and orchards, eight acres for poultry, the parkland with trout ponds, clear sparkling creeks and, later, ponds for boating and swimming, Dentonia provided an idyllic setting for the gay clan life of Massey children and grandchildren.

New Interests, New Talents

Life in those early years of the twentieth century was very good to the young Masseys, full of happy family events that colour the memory, though there were sorrows, too. They were a warm-hearted, imaginative, lively clan, sharing each others' interests and enthusiasms. Though the word "theatre" was taboo in their Methodist *milieu*, there was a stage at one end of a big room on the top floor of 550 Jarvis Street with dressing-rooms, lights and a curtain, where historical and biblical tableaux could be acted out. There were the Christmas parties at which teen-aged Vincent, as Santa Claus, would read sonorously from a big book: "I see here that Madeline slapped Denton," and Raymond, when called, answered with deliberation, "My name is Raymond Hart Massey, my grandfather's name in the *middle*." Once, secreting himself in the chimney, Vincent made his entrance through a wide fireplace before a shocked five-year-old Denton, who had been heard expressing a certain disbelief in the existence of a real Santa. Dorothy remembers Grandmother Massey's eighty-fifth birthday in 1907 (she died in 1908) when all the guests received small cut-glass vases of violets tied with violet ribbons, and there was a cake with eighty-five mauve candles.

Denton was the youngest of Walter's four children, a year old when his father died. He grew into a blond mischief who was good in church "so I can blow off when I get home." The time he shattered the glass in the observatory with a firecracker set off in a piece of drainpipe was to make an indelible impact on his memory of those days. He horrified his mother by coming home one day shorn of his hated curls, which he had had removed without maternal permission in a Yonge Street barber shop, after shovelling enough snow to pay for the haircut.

Madeline, a sensitive, imaginative child who wore her hair in a long thick braid, invented magic games called "Adventures." In shivering delight the other children would follow her around the lawns and through the trees where strange "leaf men" might be encountered and the only safety lay in dropping instantly to the ground. She also dreamed up the plays and charades endlessly performed by the children. Big boxes of dress-up clothes were kept on the third floor of Walter's Farm House at Dentonia and from these the children improvised costumes, using the lining from Aunt Lilly's mink stole, rainbow-dyed sheets, yards of bunting, a silk Swedish costume, clown suits. The same assortment was in use for years and put to every kind of creative purpose. Grey sateen in which the young Dorothy was once the hind legs of an elephant became the lining for a gipsy cloak when an older Dorothy was organizing summer theatre classes for children at Dentonia in the 1940s.

The family was close-knit, intelligent and inventive. There was no lack of spontaneous activity, and entertainments were organized over weeks of enthusiastic planning and preparation. Any excuse brought out the ham in all of them. A party "given in honour of Henry V of England's birthday" saw the grown-ups appear in a fine array of impromptu costumes, and on the lawns Diana the Huntress and Robin Hood fraternized happily with Izaak Walton, Mother Goose, Robinson Crusoe and the Queen of Hearts. The "coaching parade" of an earlier period was a memorable event in which the costumes were kept a delicious last-minute secret, and every carriage and farm vehicle was pressed into service. The elaborate decorations took the whole of one day. The procession paraded all the roadways of the estate, and Uncle John Treble played John Bull. Susan's niece Grace Carter was Ceres in a pale blue dress, her cheeks

149

rouged by rubbing with wet red *crêpe* paper; Uncle Willard and six-year-old Dorothy were Uncle Sam and Miss Canada, and Vincent appeared in blackface.

Vincent was growing into a thin, eager, intellectually curious young man who amused himself dressing his small brother Raymond in fantastic costumes and gravitated away from his father's quiet hearth to the more academically stimulating atmosphere half a block down Jarvis in the home of his friend Murray Wrong, son of Dr. George Wrong, professor of history at the University of Toronto.

In 1903, on a trip to England with his parents and Raymond, Vincent had spent a lot of his time wandering through the streets of London, riding around on the open tops of double-decker buses to the end of the line, revelling in the old city's atmosphere of history that made him feel like a long-absent son come home at last. His memories of an even earlier visit to Europe were the small personal ones of a four-year-old getting a high-buttoned boot caught in a street grating, and the panicky moments of being lost in Geneva before a kindly gendarme returned him to his mother. Now, with his mother, he went to His Majesty's Theatre to see the English actor-manager Beerbohm Tree in a magnificent performance of *Richard II*, an unforgettable experience for a sixteen-year-old who had been taught to regard the theatre as the abode of the devil.

His younger brother Raymond, though only seven at the time, has retained a touchingly tender memory of the event. It had to be a matinée (somehow Chester felt this was less *evil*), and one of the arguments Anna used to break down her solemn husband's resistance was that a Shakespearean production had been presented at the Chautauqua season only the summer before by her half-brother, Bishop John Heyl Vincent. Raymond and his father spent the afternoon at the zoo, but some of the overflow excitement got through to the little boy when his mother and his big brother came sparkling home from the show.

150

There was more glamour a few nights later when father took mother to the Covent Garden opera (that was not *theatre*), father tall and elegant in white tie and tails, mother in the beautiful new gown with the net top that Vincent had helped her choose. In Toronto Vincent would often accompany his mother in the carriage when she drove downtown to the stores. Even at sixteen his taste in clothes could guide Anna's choice.

The glamour and the gaiety of that night made a good setting against which both boys could remember their tiny vivacious mother. Only two weeks later an appendectomy proved fatal.

In the days when appendicitis was nearly always fatal she had little chance, though she was given every treatment known to the doctors of 1903. She had seemed to be well enough to continue arrangements for their return to Canada on October twenty-first but three days before the sailing date she suffered a relapse. The family moved from the hotel to a house in Hampstead, and an appendectomy was performed on November ninth. But Anna grew rapidly worse, and after she had said good night to Vincent and thanked him for the roses he had sent her that afternoon and talked a while with her husband, she became unconscious and died on November eleventh.

The nurse who had been with her throughout her illness wrote a poignant letter to Eliza Ann about her daughter-in-law, at Chester's request: "It is quite impossible for me to tell you how brave, bright and heroic Mrs. Massey was. She never once complained and her thought for everyone was most wonderful and touching. I loved Mrs. Massey very much. One could not help loving her . . . She had talked to me so much of you and her home, which she loved so dearly, and was so looking forward to her return."

"Gay, charming, vivacious Anna," said the Reverend Nathaniel Burwash sadly in a memorial address. "She was beyond charm," her elder son would remember, sixty years later.

Chester married again in 1907, his cousin, Margaret Phelps, and life in the spacious house at 519 Jarvis, though soberly happy, was unexciting, enlivened only by Chester's unfailing good humour and droll witticisms. An early illness had left him a partial invalid, and the care he took of his health was a family joke in which no one joined more heartily than Chester. "He even aired his pocket handkerchiefs," teased his sister-in-law Susan, and he cheerfully accepted the laughter every time he peeled off three overcoats one after the other as a cold day warmed up. His enjoyment of practical jokes and his sense of mimicry made him, like all the Masseys, a first-class actor in charades.

Blinding headaches often made reading difficult: his wife read to him a lot, and one of his most satisfying pleasures was to sit comfortably garbed in black velvet jacket and silently enjoy his collection of pictures in the small oak-panelled "gallery" with its leaded skylight. His life was devoted to the administration of his father's will, his association with the Methodist Church and charitable and cultural causes. His visitors included leading churchmen of North America.

Though young Vincent had a warm relationship with his father, his stepmother and his young brother, much more to his taste was the home of Dr. George Wrong, the former home of federal Liberal leader the Honourable Edward Blake, Mrs. Wrong's father. Vincent was just beginning to see the path along which he wished his life to move and which, with judgment and dignity, he followed to the ultimate pinnacle as Canada's first native-born Governor General.

Steps on this path—the University of Toronto and Balliol College, Oxford—led Vincent first, in 1913, to an appointment at the University of Toronto as lecturer in modern history and Dean of Residence at Burwash Hall, Victoria College.

In 1915 his private life saw the beginning of what he has termed "thirty-five years of complete happiness." On a couple of visits while in England to the home of the Secretary of the Rhodes Trust, Dr. G. R. (later Sir George) Parkin, Vincent had met his daughter Alice, a graceful girl with blue-grey eyes and delicately auburn hair. When she came to Canada with her father and later

152

became dean at Queen's Hall residence for women students in Toronto, the mutual attraction developed further. Students of those days got used to the sight of a lean figure struggling out of the depths of a fireside armchair when they had occasion to visit the dean's sitting-room during the evening. They were married in June, 1915, from the Kingston residence of Alice's sister Maude whose husband, William L. Grant, was a Queen's University professor. Being a wartime wedding (Vincent was a lieutenant-colonel in charge of musketry training at Camp Borden), the 8.30 A.M. ceremony was very simple, and the wedding breakfast was a hamper picnic by the roadside as the newly-weds started for their honeymoon in the Adirondacks of New York State, in a Packard that was a wedding gift from Chester. Years later Vincent was to say with touching simplicity, when a visitor commented on the wonderful life he had had, "I was most fortunate, and you see, I had *her*. No man ever had a wife more understanding, more willing to share what came. We shared a tremendous feeling of adventure. We used to laugh together when we were alone, over the small things we both thought were funny, and we had a way of teasing each other gently—we were as close a team as any two could be."

The year 1918 saw another milestone in Vincent's life and one dear to his heart: the establishment of the Massey Foundation from the assets of his grandfather's estate. In this project, the first of its kind in Canada, Vincent was advised by his cousin George Vincent, head of the Rockefeller Foundation in New York.

Under the terms of the 1896 will, the estate was to be wound up in twenty years. Vincent got his cousin to persuade Chester that a foundation would be a good thing. By preventing a possibly undiscriminating distribution of the estate's assets too rapidly, a foundation could turn it into a continuing benefaction. Accordingly a corporation called the Massey Foundation was created by federal charter, to which the assets of the estate were transferred. This conformed to the law and did not contradict the terms of the will. Chester became chairman, though his ill-health meant greater participation by Vincent in the administration of the Foundation. One of its first undertakings was the completion of Hart House, Toronto University's social and cultural centre for male students, the construction of which had been interrupted by the First World War. In recent years it has retreated a little from its masculine aloofness, and women students are now allowed certain Hart House privileges.

In an offshoot of this project, the Hart House Theatre, Vincent was to earn a reputation as an actor often said to outdo his famous brother Raymond's. "As a lecturer he always wore the same expression," said one of his former students. "But in *Pantaloon* he played the part of the clown, a part which no one would have dreamed that Vincent Massey of all people could play . . . He was inimitable." Some twenty years later the small daughter of Lester Pearson, First Secretary to the Canadian High Commission in London, would be enthralled at a Christmas party by Vincent's savage portrayal of Captain Bligh.

After Chester's death in 1926, at the age of seventy-six, Vincent became chairman of the Massey Foundation, and in the public mind its benefactions have come to be accepted as Vincent's personal generosity. Some of his Massey cousins resent the acclaim he receives. "It should be known as the *Hart* Massey Foundation," said one of them. "It's not Vincent's money—it's our grandfather's."

In 1925 Vincent was invited to join Mackenzie King's Liberal cabinet as minister without portfolio. He failed to win a seat in the election, having chosen to contest the riding in which he lived. It had been solidly Conservative for twenty years and insisted on remaining so. In the interests of a political career he had already terminated his association with Massey-Harris, where he had been a competent, if not venturesome, president from 1921 to 1925. This marked the end of the family's direct associa-

154

tion with the company, which in 1958 became known as Massey-Ferguson after its amalgamation with the extensive British farm-machinery business built up by Harry Ferguson.

In 1926 Vincent went to Washington as the first Canadian Minister to the United States. In 1930 his acceptance of the post of High Commissioner in London was cancelled by the defeat of Mackenzie King's government, and until 1935, when King was able to offer it again, Vincent filled the years with travel. He met Mussolini in Rome, was in Madrid when the republic was proclaimed, visited the Far East. He attended a variety of international conferences and developed his private estate, Batterwood, near Port Hope, Ontario.

Meanwhile, life at Dentonia Park Farm was following its pleasant privileged pattern, and Walter's children were growing up under Susan's firm but gentle direction. There was always something going on, visits from aunts and uncles and cousins, week-end parties, groups of people being entertained at garden parties on the estate. "There was seldom any bickering among us," one of them recalls nostalgically, "and none of us took offence easily. We had good-natured fun getting a rise out of each other, but we were all very congenial, sharing the same sense of humour and the same kind of imagination."

Hearty Uncle Willard would come to visit, before he took up permanent residence at Dentonia, and taught the children fascinating games: how to toss green apples from pointed sticks into the pond below the knoll, how to bait their own hooks and clean the trout they caught on Saturday for Sunday morning's breakfast and, using a punt because there was no canoe, how to paddle silently, as the Indians did. They played hide-and-seek among the haycocks, rode bicycles round the flower beds, put up tents on the knoll, ran stamping over the bridge across the ravine to visit the deer pen.

There was the excitement of summer house parties organized by the older ones, Vincent and Ruth, with groups of handsome debonair young men (Dorothy thought one of them named Arthur Goulding was particularly nice), and bevies of chattering young ladies in many petticoats under starched white dresses that had an awful attraction for bugs. Curly-headed Denton liked trotting along beside a group of them, basking in the attention he got. Once one of the young ladies climbed up the water tower and asked a startled Chester to catch her when she jumped. They played croquet, tennis and golf, and went for excursions in the tally-ho and early-model motor car, and there were "official" tournaments for family and friends sponsored by Ruth's Dentonia Athletic Club, when field days were held and cups presented for golf, tennis, jumping and bicycle races. Ruth and Vincent edited a little paper, *The Dentonia Telltale*, for distribution in the family circle. Lost personal articles were impounded for claim and purchased back by their owners at a weekly auction. Twelve-year-old Dorothy, who was responsible for keeping the accounts, suffered sleepless nights from time to time over columns that added up a couple of cents short.

Raymond, a rather lonely little boy who was often sickly and sometimes stayed at his father's summer home across from the Farm House, came over to mess up the girls' toy room, but was forgiven when he convulsed everyone by his performances in charades and tableaux. His voice and Madeline's (only a few months older) would echo back and forth over the sloping drop of the driveway between their two homes as they called to one another:

"Come over and play with me, Ma-a-adeline?"

"After a whi-ile, Ray-mie!"

Prim and proper in their best dresses and importantly ensconced in the family box, the little girls would sit enchanted by the music when on special occasions they were allowed to attend concerts at Massey Hall, like their older cousins Vincent and Ruth whose attendance at the concerts was an event especially treasured because they were allowed to stay up late.

Dorothy, big-eyed and hero-worshipping, would take flowers

from the conservatory to present to the stars backstage. When she was twelve, she arranged a special entertainment for the family in honour of Caruso's birthday, with a programme prepared in her neat round hand listing "Address by Miss Dorothy Massey" to follow the intermission. She sent a copy to Caruso. He returned a signed photograph.

She adored Schumann-Heink and Madame Gadski and disapproved of Melba, perhaps not surprisingly, as she must have been a bit overdressed even by prima-donna standards. The press reported next day:

Her costume was an exquisite gown slightly draped and with a short pointed train. The material was Rose du Barri satin with medallions embroidered over it in gold bullion; the shoulder straps were of pearls and the long pointed sleeves of tulle ended in large tassels of pearls and diamonds, on the left side of the bodice was a bow of black velvet, with ends to the hem of the skirt also ending in the beautiful tassels of pearl. With this was worn a stomacher of diamonds studded with enormous pearls and fastened round her neck with a diamond chain. She also had on a rope of pearls. In her hair was a curled black osprey [*sic*] held with a diamond ornament and circular diamond clasps secured a black velvet ribbon surrounding her head.

Special events highlighted every season, the important trivia that build the happiest memories. Before the Toronto Exhibition each fall, Dorothy anxiously watched the sky and agonized over the paper doll stuck in her window whose chemically treated skirt would change through pink and violet to the blue that said the weather would be fine. The family would drive in the carriage to the exhibition and visit the cattle from Dentonia Park Farm in wooden stalls tied with goldenrod and strewn with tanbark. It was thrilling to sit in the grandstand and see the white-jacketed attendants lead the cattle into the ring wearing yellow-bordered white blankets with DPF initials.

In summer the young folk walked to and from the bathhouse in white bathrobes to swim and splash in the ninety-foot pool and slide squealing down the chute. In winter they skied and

157

tobogganed and skated. Dorothy's knee acquired a scar to mark the time when Raymond let her go too soon in a game of "whip," and the weather was often so cold that the Victrola froze, and the music with it.

At thirteen and already six feet tall, Denton led a Bible class at Hope Church in East Toronto—foreshadowing the religious fervour that would make him a national figure in later years. The children's education and manners were polished by European trips, a Mediterranean cruise for Susan's health, a year in Munich where Dorothy studied the piano. Here they were joined by Ruth and her husband, who was engaged in postgraduate medical work. Ruth had been married in 1910 to Dr. Harold Tovell, one of the first Toronto doctors to work with X-rays, and she had worn Aunt Lillian's veil and a long-sleeved dress made from the skirt of her mother's wedding gown.

In 1908 the City Dairy had taken over the cattle management at the farm. Its operation was discontinued in 1913 and the big barn was taken down. In the same year Susan sold the town house on Jarvis Street. The Farm House built by Walter was demolished, and on its site she began to build the big house she called "Susan's Folly," but the war intervened and it could not be completed until 1918. Chesterfield Inn, Chester's summer home, had been winterized: the family lived here, and in Rest Cottage, formerly the farm foreman's house and after that a rest home for the mission deaconnesses.

In 1916 Ruth was back at Dentonia with her husband and first child, Walter, when her eighteen-year-old sister Dorothy was married to Dr. Arthur Goulding, whom she had known since childhood.

Dr. Goulding, a graduate of the University of Toronto, of Oxford (in political science) and of Harvard Medical School, had recently returned to Canada from England on sick leave from the air force. The wedding was held in the billiard room, its glass windows opening onto the tops of the trees around the house, and Dorothy in a satin gown with inset panel of lace from Aunt Lillian's dress came down the wide stairs on her uncle Chester's arm. Madeline was bridesmaid, and the ceremony saw Denton, now sixteen, in his first morning coat. Twenty-year-old Raymond, handsome in uniform and temporarily invalided home from the fighting front in Europe, was usher. He had suffered shock and a wounded hand when his dug-out had been blown up while he was serving in Belgium as a lieutenant with the Canadian Field Artillery. Immediately after the wedding Dorothy and her husband left for New York via Boston, and sailed for England in a ship blacked-out against the danger of prowling U-boats. Discovering when he reached London that he had been invalided out of the air force, Arthur Goulding worked for three months at St. Bartholomew's Hospital in London before returning to Harvard for further medical studies.

For some years Charles Albert's five children had been estranged from the rest of the family after bringing a lawsuit to contest their grandfather's will in which an out-of-court settlement was made. Vincent, in his teens, arranged a not-too-successful dinner party to try to reunite the family. As time went by, the early bitterness passed; Winnie, and her sisters Jennie and Bessie who had also grown into remarkably beautiful girls, sometimes visited Dentonia, along with Arnold, their brother Arthur's son. Arnold's friendship with Raymond, only a year older, had done much to break the ice. Tragedy had not finished with Charles Albert's family, however. His wife Jessie had died in 1894, after only seven years of marriage to Haydn Horsey. Both his sons were to die violently, Charles Albert (Bert) shot on his doorstep by a housemaid, and Arthur, depressed over his mortgage business in the 1930s, by his own hand.

Into the Twentieth Century

At a time when the prime space was devoted to war news the death in February, 1915, of thirty-four-year-old Bert Massey, a salesman with York Motors, made the front pages of Toronto newspapers. An eighteen-year-old housemaid, Carrie Davis, who had brooded all day Monday, February eighth, over what she claimed were advances attempted by Bert the day before, opened the front door as he came up the steps to his house in the evening, and shot him point-blank with his own gun.

Bert's wife was on a brief visit to the United States and had asked Carrie, who had been with the Masseys since her arrival from England two years earlier, to take care of "the master" and their fourteen-year-old son while she was away. On the previous Friday evening Carrie had waited at table for a party given by Bert, which had broken up at midnight. Saturday had been uneventful, Carrie said at the trial, Mr. Massey had thanked her for her work at the Friday party, offered her a dollar to pay a woman for extra help, which she refused as not necessary, and gave her a shamrock ring made of pearls. Then, she said, he kissed her, and later made improper advances which she resisted. In the afternoon she had gone to visit a sister who lived nearby, and had been halted in her story of what had happened by the presence of a young visitor.

She did, however, mention the kisses to her brother-in-law and wondered if it would be better not to go back, but her brother-in-law reminded her of her promise to Mrs. Massey to look after the master. She had then, as the *Evening Telegram* reported her statement at her trial, "gone on playing with her sister's children and forgot afterwards to tell her sister what happened." It was an extraordinary lapse of memory in view of her later action.

Bert was visiting friends on Sunday evening, and there was no further incident between him and the girl, nor did she see him in the morning, for she called him when breakfast was ready and then went down to stand by the cellar door until he had departed for the office.

All day long her mind remained obsessed with Bert's attempt to embrace her, by which act she said afterwards with appalling innocence, "He ruined my life." At just after six o'clock the paper boy called for his money, and Carrie explained he would have to get it from Mr. Massey. The boy asked if that was Mr. Massey coming down the street now.

"I guess it was then I lost control of myself, and I thought of what he was going to do, and it frightened me," said Carrie, sole witness at the trial of what he had done or might have been going to do. "Everything was misty before me . . . I thought of defending myself, and I went for the revolver that was hanging in the little boy's room."

Bert's fourteen-year-old son, a third-generation Charles Albert, had fixed up the gun, a .32 revolver, and used it for shooting ground-hogs in the country. Carrie had learned from him how to load it and had seen it fired. The grim story was unfolded at the trial in her own words. "She gave her answers," reported the *Evening Telegram*, which had sponsored a fund for her defence, "clearly and distinctly, and without the slightest sign of nervousness."

She went upstairs, she said, "and took the revolver and six cartridges. It held five and the other one I took to my bedroom . . . I put them in the revolver as I was going downstairs, thinking all the time that he would do me harm. . . . I got two steps when the door opened and I fired . . . I said, 'You have ruined my life.' Then I shot him . . . I remember firing again on the doorstep . . . I ran up to my room. I did not realize that I had

161

Kinsale Association Library.

shot Mr. Massey. I remember faintly writing two letters . . . to my sister and a friend . . . and did several things up there."

At an emotional trial two weeks later she was acquitted of murder after the jury had been out for half an hour. The presiding judge, Chief Justice Sir William Mulock, praised her for her devotion. "Evidently she is a person of a supersensitive, conscientious nature," he declared. "Her pledge to her mistress not to absent herself from the house when the master was absent was a pledge she felt bound to keep, and in this age I think it is an encouraging and pleasant thing to find some person so devoted to respecting one's promise as the prisoner seems to have been."

Even, one is tempted to ask, if it means shooting the master?

"Up till the time Mrs. Massey went on holidays, there was nothing in Mr. Massey's conduct so far as she was concerned to which she could object, the girl said," reported the *Telegram*.

"Even if Massey had forgotten himself," crown counsel had commented drily at the beginning of the trial, "the death sentence seemed to be fairly severe."

Bert's son, Charles Albert, had been in the basement engaged in his hobby of glass-blowing, and had heard nothing of the shooting until he came upstairs and was met by a policeman in the hall. In his later career he showed his heritage of Massey intelligence and initiative. He grew up to become an Osgoode Hall Law School medalist, married Audrey Hewitt, sister of sportscaster Foster Hewitt, and was president of Lever Brothers in Canada when he retired in 1958.

The war over, the Massey men came back to civilian life.

Toward the end of the war Vincent had been lent to the secretariat of the War Committee of the cabinet in Ottawa; when hostilities ended, he became secretary, later director, of the Government Repatriation Committee, before returning to private life and a few years in the family business.

162

Raymond, who as a lieutenant in the Canadian Field Artillery had been wounded at Ypres in 1916, had gone to Siberia on active service with the Canadian Expeditionary Force, after a year with the British Military Mission to the United States as military instructor in trench warfare and gunnery at Yale and Princeton. To relieve the tedium of the year in Siberia, he organized and took part in a minstrel show that kept the troops from utter boredom. He came home to a brief period with Massey-Harris, and finally broke down his father's resistance to the idea of a professional stage career. Raymond's talent for acting had been demonstrated since the days of school dramatics. It was far too competent to be restricted by outdated puritanism. Chester gave a reluctant consent to his plans, asking only that he should not "practise" on Sundays. His first professional part was in Eugene O'Neill's *In The Zone* in London in 1922, so Chester lived to see the beginning of his younger son's rise to fame in his chosen field. In the future nearly everyone in the world would know the name of Raymond Massey, stage and film star, famous for two particular roles: Abraham Lincoln on stage and screen, and Dr. Gillespie on television. Altogether his roles have numbered close to two hundred.

Arnold, Arthur's son and eldest grandson of Charles Albert, had served with the Canadian Army, the Royal Naval Air Service and the Royal Air Force, and was decorated with the Air Force Cross. Back in Toronto, he entered an investment firm, eventually becoming a vice-president.

Denton, who had joined up as soon as he turned eighteen in June, 1918, and had seen a few months' service with the Yale Battery, entered the Massachusetts Institute of Technology after the war ended. A big handsome outgoing sentimental young man who carried his father's Swiss watch—Hart's wedding present to his third son—and used his father's Bible daily, he fell in love at first sight with Esther Jeralds of New Haven, Connecticut, and became engaged in 1921 at a Dentonia house party, when he clasped around her wrist a facsimile of the Hawaiian bracelet given to his mother by his father. They were married in January, 1922, but appendicitis put Denton into hospital, forced postponement of a world trip, and delayed the completion of his MIT course. He came back to Toronto in 1924 with the MIT engineering degree of S.B. and worked for a few years at Massey-Harris, starting, as all young men did who were destined for executive posts, with a term of work in the various shops.

The boss of one of the shops to which he was assigned had trained many such young men and the Massey name failed to connect in his mind with that of the firm. Surprised when Denton asked permission to use the wash basin in the office, he gave a gruff "No. Wash outside with the other men." A few days later, asking permission to be a little late next morning, Denton was emphatically informed that his pay would be docked accordingly.

"Why do you expect to be late?" his boss asked.

"Uh—my wife and I have been invited to dine with the Prince of Wales," explained Denton diffidently, to his boss's huge amusement. Arriving late next morning, Denton was duly reprimanded, informed of his wage cut and sent to his post with a muffled guffaw. The boss was still laughing when he glanced casually through the morning's paper in an off moment—and went cold. "Guests at the Prince of Wales' reception and dance at the York Club," he read, "included Mr. and Mrs. Denton Massey. Mrs. Massey danced twice with His Royal Highness."

The boss beckoned over a colleague. "He's one of the *Massey* Masseys," he whispered frantically. "What will I *do*?"

"Don't do a thing," his colleague advised. "He wouldn't want you to treat him any differently."

"And you know," said the workshop boss in telling the story, "I didn't, and he didn't, and we've been friends ever since."

Denton rose to become assistant superintendent of the Toronto works, left to preside over his own advertising agency, and then successfully contested the federal election of 1935 as a Conservative candidate for Toronto-Greenwood. He held the seat in 1940 and 1945 but did not contest the 1949 election. Friends feel that a

164

promising political career was thrown away in favour of a deeper interest, for alongside—perhaps ahead of—all others was Denton's role as leader of the York Bible Class for Young Men.

It started in February, 1925, with nineteen young men in the basement of Hope Church Sunday School, itself a gift from Susan in Walter's memory. Asked to lead the group, Denton specified that its members must work with him and show their interest by bringing a friend to the first meeting he would lead. The original six turned up with two friends each. By the end of 1931, following what was up to that time, the biggest indoor religious gathering in Canada's history (on December thirteenth) when only seventeen thousand of thirty-seven thousand people could get into Maple Leaf Gardens, York Bible Class membership had risen to nearly two thousand five hundred, and the class had moved its meeting place to successively larger buildings, ending in the two-thousand-five-hundred-seat Yorkminster Church.

To the class Denton brought his gifts of personality, administration and fervour. Like his idolized father, he had the ability to reach his audience and bring Bible history alive. The first broadcast of a Bible class on the North American continent was arranged by Denton over station CKCL on September thirteenth, 1925: soon the whole of Ontario and many United States centres were listening in. On February twentieth, 1927, Denton's first broadcast over station CFRB brought him back to his grandfather's home at 515 Jarvis Street. The CFRB studio was in what used to be Aunt Lilly's sun porch, and the announcer who put him on the air was a young man named Ernest Bushnell, later Director General of Programmes for the CBC.

A more cynical age tends to look back with some reservations about his sincerity on this handsome privileged young man and his easy ability to step into the limelight. But hard-headed businessmen of today who were close to him in those days still have undertones of hero-worship in their voices when they speak of Denton Massey, and it is difficult, meeting him, to avoid the belief that his convictions have always been genuine, that he tried to use his gifts to the glory of God and not to the glory of Denton Massey.

A fellow class-member said thirty years later:

Denton was the biggest-hearted chap alive. He was dedicated and democratic, and a sucker for everyone in need. He would speak anywhere and fill churches and halls, refusing to charge and often contributing. I remember once accepting a cheque on his behalf for one of his engagements and being despatched, in cold silence, to mail it back from the first stop the train made on the journey home. He literally gave away thousands of dollars. He bought coats for needy people, and I've seen him slip as much as five hundred dollars to pay some man's fine for him. He was the kind of person who brought out the best basic qualities in every one of us. We were all too busy doing things those days to worry about the depression.

When World War II came, Denton joined the Royal Canadian Air Force as a pilot officer, spent several years overseas and retired as a group-captain with an OBE. Various enterprises followed. His own automobile dealerships and agencies took him to Europe and the United States. He was associated with the atomic energy division of the American Machine and Foundry Company, and the setting up of its Canadian company, AMF Atomics (Canada) Limited, with head offices and factory located at Port Hope, almost next door to his family's early Canadian home.

But his feeling for religion won in the end. In 1960, at sixty, he was ordained as an Anglican priest. His first charge was the church at Point Edward, near Sarnia, Ontario. In 1963 he moved to the Church of the Holy Saviour in Waterloo, Ontario. This, he feels, is "the most important work of my life."

From Point Edward he once wrote to his cousin Raymond, mentioning that church duties interfered with his viewing of the TV programme "Dr. Kildare," in which Raymond was playing his famous role of Dr. Gillespie. "I've given you up for Lent," he said. A photograph of Raymond came back inscribed, "A Lenten abstention affectionately greets the Rector of St. Paul's." Denton hung it on the wall of the rectory study.

166

Following the First World War, Vincent Massey had acquired an estate—now four hundred acres—near Port Hope. There, in rolling wooded countryside where the Ganaraska River widens to form a little lake, and an old mill from around 1800 still grinds feed grain, Vincent and his wife Alice lovingly planned a comfortable, English-eighteenth-century-style red brick house, which they called Batterwood House ("a wood on a gentle slope") in which, over the next twenty-two years, the longest period they would be able to spend together with their two boys, Lionel (born 1916) and Hart (born 1918), were the years between 1930 and 1935, after Vincent's return from his Washington appointment and before going to London as Canada's High Commissioner in 1935.

In his public life he was supported by the devoted assistance of his wife, particularly during the war years. It was Alice Massey who established the Canadian Officers' Club in London to provide lunch in a home atmosphere for service personnel. The Beaver Club, for other ranks, also received the keen support of the Masseys. "An absolutely first-class cook," in her husband's words, she knew how to make the best possible use of rationed food. Every day she went on duty to serve a variety of food that was often delivered to the club by Vincent after being cooked by Alice in a large container over the gas-ring in the bathroom. At a time when one son was a prisoner of war and the other seriously wounded—Lionel, an officer in the King's Royal Rifles, in Greece, and Hart, a flight-lieutenant in the Royal Canadian Air Force, in an air raid in England—Alice Massey was writing letters of sympathy to bereaved Canadian families, shopping for soldiers wanting to send gifts home, planning concert entertainments, writing to the families of men resting at Garnons, the country home supported by the Massey Foundation as a convalescent home for Canadian officers. She even arranged wedding receptions in her own London flat.

In 1946, after he had retired as High Commissioner, Vincent

and Alice returned to Canada and spent a year on a cross-Canada tour. Vincent made speeches, renewed his knowledge of his native land, produced the book *On Being Canadian*. In 1947 he was elected Chancellor of the University of Toronto. From 1949 to 1951 he served as chairman of the Royal Commission on Natural Development in the Arts, Letters and Sciences, which produced a remarkably readable five-hundred-page report and suggested the institution that eventually became the Canada Council.

In July, 1950, Alice Massey died at Batterwood House after a long period of failing health, eighteen months before her husband became the first Canadian Governor General of Canada, though she lived long enough to know that his name had been suggested for the appointment.

It must have been a lonely triumph for Vincent without his wife to share it. She would have delighted in the adventurous symbolism of the time when Vincent flew to the North Pole and dropped a canister containing, among other things, the Governor General's flag. She would have been proud of the distinction with which he presided at events of formal dignity. And there were moments they would have recalled with happy private laughter: the time, for instance, when a shrill ten-year-old voice announced above the babel of chatter after the Governor General had addressed a group of school children, "He's a living *doll*!"

History sometimes happily foreshadows an interesting future event. On a bright October day in the year 1862, amid a cheering crowd of local residents and the noise of "cannon and explosive signals", the Right Honourable Charles Stanley, Viscount Monck, Governor General of British North America, had stepped from a train at the Ontario town of Port Hope onto a dais decorated with evergreens and flowers and hung with the Royal Standard, the Union Jack, the Cross of St. George and a banner with the ancient arms of Ireland, gravely listened to an address by the local mayor, inspected cavalry and infantry volunteers and

168

was cheered back into his carriage to resume his journey after the short stopover.

Almost a hundred years later, in July, 1959, the Queen of Canada would herself come to the same small town, to visit her personal representative, another governor general of Canada, in his private residence located about four miles from the railway station where the townspeople of Port Hope had greeted his predecessor.

For three days the Royal Standard flew over Batterwood House, and the cassocks of royal scarlet now worn by the clergy and choir at St. Mark's in Port Hope continue to honour the attendance at Sunday service of Queen Elizabeth and Prince Philip: an ancient custom specially revived for an unusual occasion.

Few critical voices have been raised to denigrate Vincent Massey's performance as Governor General, which has been acclaimed as a significant achievement of an outstanding Canadian. He brought to it the strengths and weaknesses of a complex personality: "an unusual mixture of generosity and vanity, of intellect and determination," said *Canada Month*, discussing his part in the controversial Massey College.

There is no doubt that he enjoyed the role. "I think Vincent had a real desire for power," said his cousin Ruth Tovell. "I don't mean, to misuse power, not in any tyrannical sense, but I think he liked very much to be top dog." But he used his privilege with dignity and to good purpose. "He made the office the symbol of the nation: the centre of the unspoken aspirations, the mood, the tempo of public life," said John Saywell, then associate professor of history, University of Toronto. "Historians of the future might well conclude that of all his services to Canada those years as Governor General from 1952 to 1959 were his greatest." Dr. Eugene Forsey, one of those who feared that sectionalism and denominationalism might develop from the appointment of a Canadian as Governor General, was able to say afterwards, "I think the chances of it now developing are much less because of the distinguished work that Mr. Massey did."

His long-time friend and fellow-student Frank Underhill, for thirty years a history professor at the University of Toronto, who has been honestly critical of what he has felt was a too complete identification "with the manners and values of a particular English social group," ended a review of Vincent's autobiography in 1963: "While remaining critical of some of his political enthusiasms, I wish that we could produce more Vincent Masseys."

At Dentonia Park "Susan's Folly" was completed in 1918 and the good life, under Susan Massey's matriarchal leadership, was repeating itself for another generation, the children of Walter Massey's four children. The grandchildren grew up with careful supervision and the same clan pride, the family activities at Dentonia interrupted only by schooling in Canada and Europe. Grandmother Susan—who wore widow's weeds (mauve in summer) to the day of her death in 1938, in her seventy-seventh year—held memorable Sunday luncheons for the grandchildren, in batches according to age. Sometimes, when their parents were away, Dorothy-Jane Goulding and her sister Susan stayed in the big house. (Grandmother's mauve bedroom was extremely glamorous, with enormous twin beds and a mauve clock, a bathroom with a bath big enough to drown in—and even mauve toilet-paper.) There were swimming and skating parties, and the garden parties Susan arranged for charitable causes; and always, being Masseys, the excitement of dressing up, acting out charades, tableaux and plays. Taboos against the theatre had gradually disappeared with the years: Raymond had seen to that.

So the great-great-great-grandchildren of the farmer, Daniel, who came into Canada a hundred and fifty odd years before to carve with his own hands a living from the virgin woodlands, reaped the harvest of their ancestors' industry and energy.

170

The Masseys of today, though they can be proud of their fore-bears, have not rested on the laurels of the past. While many of them are living lives of quiet personal activity, with family and community interests, others have reached out farther and become public figures to varying degrees. Vincent's elder son Lionel, who was secretary to his father during the latter's term as Governor General, became associate director of the Royal Ontario Museum until his tragically early death in August, 1965. Vincent's younger son, Hart, is an award-winning architect living in Ottawa. Raymond's tall eldest son Geoffrey, also an architect, lives in Vancouver. With his colleague Arthur Erickson, he was placed first of seventy-one entrants in the 1963 competition for the new Simon Fraser University at Burnaby, B.C.

Walter's eldest daughter, Ruth Tovell, herself a writer—a detective novel in the 1930s and two scholarly art studies, *Flemish Artists of the Valois Court* (1950) and *Roger van der Weyden and the Flemalle Enigma* (1955)—left four sons who ably exemplify the Massey vitality. Walter, the eldest, is curator of geology at the Royal Ontario Museum. Freeman serves as Canadian Ambassador to Peru. Harold is director of Woman's Hospital in New York. The youngest, and only bachelor, Vincent, taught English at Upper Canada College and has been winning laurels as a producer of some of the CBC's best documentaries.

Dorothy and her tall, distinguished, grey-bearded husband, Dr. Arthur Goulding, still live in the roomy house they built at Dentonia Park, hidden in a pleasant oasis of trees on the corner lot she had picked out for herself as a child. Dr. Goulding has been retired for some years after a busy and varied career in medicine, serving in several hospitals and lecturing at the University of Toronto. Their four daughters were educated in Canada, England and Europe, and the family travelled a good deal through the years.

At Dentonia, when Dorothy was director of the Toronto Children Players from 1933 to 1958, she often entertained groups of children to perform and rehearse. "She can do wonders with sets and lighting," someone commented, "and acts as her own carpenter, painter and upholsterer." Many of the costumes the children used came from the big attic boxes of Dorothy's own childhood, and by one of those happy coincidences the young man who had done the flower friezes in the pastel-coloured bedrooms of Walter Massey's Farm House half a century earlier turned up as the old man who sometimes helped Walter's daughter with the stage sets.

The Gouldings' eldest daughter, Helen, is Mrs. Hugh Lloyd, a biologist at the University of Manitoba and busily involved with her family, local politics, ballet and other cultural interests. Susan, the third Goulding daughter, made a name for herself as Susan Fletcher on radio and stage, with documentaries and monologues. For some years she has lived in Jamaica, in charge of a staff of thirty-five and seven miles from the nearest telephone, with her third husband, Alan Keeling, who breeds horses. Dorothy-Jane, the youngest Goulding girl and wife of actor William Needles, was for years director of the CBC's "Kindergarten of the Air." She maintains her town house in winter, and with the help of her five children and a hired hand she runs a farm in summer, involving herself with tireless energy in every community activity, including the local choir, the Women's Institute and the rural school. She also edits material for the CBC.

Denton's eldest daughter, Elizabeth Caroline (Betty), married Louis Breithaupt of Kitchener, Ontario. The eldest of her three boys, another Louis, is the fifth of the name in Canada. Denton's other daughter, Marilyn, lives in Virginia where her husband Stewart Treviranus, a member of the Canadian equestrian team in the 1952 Olympics, trains hunters on a one-hundred-and-ten-acre farm. Denton's youngest child, his son Walter Edward Hart, is a promising Montreal actor, married to English actress Anne Butler.

Raymond continues his career in Hollywood. He became an American citizen in March, 1944, and lives with his third wife, Dorothy Ludington Whitney, whom he married in 1939. Daniel and Anna, his two children by his second wife, English actress Adrienne Allen, both brought up in England, are making a name for themselves in the world of theatre, too. Daniel has had many stage and film successes in England and recently played the male lead in the Broadway musical *She Loves Me*. Anna is a top performer on the London stage. For her first professional role in *The Reluctant Débutante* in 1955, her father flew over from the United States. Anna, who had not noticed him out front, found him waiting for her backstage after the performance.

In Oakville, Ontario, eighty-four-year-old Bessie Irene (now Mrs. E. S. Glassco), the "baby darling" of Charles Albert's ill-starred family, still cherishes her memories of a beloved grandfather. Her son by her first marriage, Dr. Arthur Armstrong, head of the laboratories at Mountain Sanatorium in Hamilton, an Oxford M.D. who worked for several years with Dr. Banting, is another whose achievements are part of the Massey heritage. And Charles Albert's grandson Arnold, a Toronto investment dealer, the eldest son of the eldest son of the eldest son, has a son and grandson of his own to carry on the line—Arnold Dewey Massey, who was married by Denton in 1961 and makes his home in Winnipeg, and Arnold Charles, born in September 1964.

Hart's vigorous initiative still lives in his descendants; his fortune, as he wished, still works for the common good. One of its latest benefactions is the two-million-dollar Massey College, controversial and striking in appearance, for postgraduate male students at the University of Toronto. It was opened in October, 1963, at a ceremony to which few of Hart's descendants received an invitation. Through all the Masseys runs a thread of pride in their ancestry, though the various branches have drawn apart and the present generation is often remote from the older members.

The house at 515 Jarvis Street, where Hart upheld the stern Methodist principles of total abstinence from liquor and worldly pleasures, is now reconstructed in period decor as a restaurant for sophisticated diners, and the master-bedroom suite upstairs where the Duke and Duchess of York did *not* sleep—despite the legend—is the Bombay Bicycle Club, vaguely oriental with dim lights, brass lamps, straw matting and statues of Buddha, where cocktails are served by attractive sari-clad occidental maidens who have never seen India.

Hart Massey and his daughter Lillian would be aghast, but most of Hart's descendants are among the sophisticates and would not mind at all.

174

PICKERING TOWNSHIP PUBLIC LIBRARY
ROUGE HILL

PLEASE USE FRONT POCKET

971.06
Masse-G

Gillen, Mollie
    The Masseys; founding family